CW00829289

Dear Mary

Thought you might
enjoy reading
through this!

All our love

Rich, Helen
xx
xx

+ Jarvah ☺

Scott Cam's
Home
maintenance
for knuckleheads

To my darling wife Ann and my children Charlie, Bill and Sarah for their love and support — and for letting me go to the pub.

Published by Murdoch Books®, a division of Murdoch Magazines Pty Ltd.

Murdoch Books® Australia, GPO Box 1203, Sydney NSW 2001

Phone: + 612 4352 7000   Fax: + 612 4352 7026

Murdoch Books UK Limited, 1 Ferry House, 51–57 Lacy Road, Putney, London SW15 1PR

Phone: + 44 (0) 20 8355 1480   Fax: + 44 (0) 20 8355 1499

Chief Executive: Juliet Rogers

Publisher: Kay Scarlett

Concept and Design: Marylouise Brammer

Photographer: Suzie Mitchell

Editor and Project Manager: Sarah Baker

Illustrator: Genevieve Huard

Production: Janis Barbi

Editorial director: Diana Hill

Printed by Midas Printing (Asia) Ltd. Printed in China.

National Library of Australia Cataloguing-in-Publication Data:

Cam, Scott. Home maintenance for knuckleheads. Includes index.

ISBN 1 74045 259 3. 1. Dwelling - Maintenance and repair - Amateurs' manuals. 1. Title. 643.7

Acknowledgments: The author and publisher wish to thank Scott van Houten of Eastern Suburbs Instant Glass, phone (02) 9365 7444, for supplying glass; the publican of Scott's favourite pub; and the obliging blokes on the Table of Knowledge.

Scott Cam's HOME maintenance for knuckleheads

MURDOCH
B O O K S

Contents

Introduction

There really are too many sensitive New Age guys out there these days and too many girls looking after these blokes. The only place for a SNAG is between two bits of white bread with a pile of tommy and heaps of salt.

It's time to stand up and be counted. Go back to the old days where blokes were blokes, when everyone had a shed with the full tool kit. If there was a problem around the house, Mum wouldn't get on the phone and call for help, she'd have a go.

As soon as there was a drama, Dad would go straight to the shed, sort the problem, and all the kids would look up at him with admiration.

This little book is going to be the start of the revolution. It's about time we all had a good ol' fashioned T-bone, two eggs and chips and black sauce — skip the pasta. The SNAG is old news.

So if you see someone talking baby talk to the cat...clip him or her around the ear, organise a working bee at a mate's place, have a barbie — better still, build it first — then cook a big lump of rump, 40 snags and burn the crap out of them,

serve them up black and if anyone complains, tell 'em about the revolution — we don't serve eggplant any more.

So having said all that, this is not a cookbook. First up you'll need tools, and the right dress code — an old flanno shirt, stubbies (or old footy shorts will do) and elastic-sided work boots.

Don't panic. I'm not going to show you how to build an Edwardian dining room table. This is the troubleshooting book for everyday problems around the house — for knuckleheads. Its setup is easy to understand and easy to follow.

The chapters are broken up into trades, like 'Carpentry' and 'Plumbing'. And each chapter is broken up into jobs — the first job in the chapter on carpentry is 'Job 1: Bouncing floorboard'.

The jobs are laid out exactly how the house was built, so in 'Carpentry' the first job is about your piers under the house and your floors, and the last job is in your roof. In 'Plumbing' the first job is about the meter (where the water starts) and the last job is in the guttering.

So load up with the flanno and nail bag and get stuck into it.

WHAT TO WEAR

If you're going to fix things around the house, you have to look the part. In summer, wear a flanno shirt (cut the sleeves off at the elbow), work shorts (make sure they've been washed 15 times before their first outing), one pair of footy socks (your team of choice — 'Go the Roosters!') and elastic-sided brown work boots (never wear black ones — they're for mechanics and black tie functions). In winter, the same applies, but you could try a newer flanno shirt with long sleeves for a bit of warmth. A trusty site manager (your dog) adds to your credibility.

old flanno shirt

well worn
work shorts

faithful dog

elastic-sided
work boots

TOP ROW (LEFT TO RIGHT): HANDSAW, COMBINATION SQUARE, CARPENTERS PENCIL, TAPE MEASURE, HACKSAW, DRILL BIT SET (STEEL AND TIMBER). MIDDLE ROW: NAIL PUNCH, SLOT-HEAD SCREWDRIVERS, MASONRY BITS, PHILLIPS-HEAD SCREWDRIVERS, POWER DRILL. BOTTOM ROW: LEVEL.

TOOLS

Your tools should be like your family — well looked after, well loved and shown off at every possible opportunity. One tip: make sure you buy quality and they'll last a lifetime.

TOP ROW: **NAIL BAG.** MIDDLE ROW (LEFT TO RIGHT): **CLAW HAMMER,** 25 MM **CHISEL, STANLEY KNIFE, CAULKING GUN, SHIFTING SPANNER, MULTI GRIPS.**

Carpentry

Many famous people have been carpenters —
Harrison Ford, Jesus's dad, Elvis...Carpentry is the
first trade. Carpenters are intelligent, strong,
sensitive to the needs of others. They're gifted,
almost artistic workhorses who never shy away from
a task, no matter how hard or big or small. Once
you can master the art of working
with wood (or fake it), you've got
the world at your feet, so good
luck — and remember, if you
can't be one, make sure
you look the part.

Job 1 BOUNCING FLOORBOARD

Problem WHEN YOU WALK ACROSS THE ROOM, THE CHINA CABINET RATTLES — A COMMON PROBLEM IN OLDER HOMES. I ALWAYS REMEMBER MY DEAR OLD GRANNY'S HOUSE USED TO SHAKE AND RATTLE AS YOU WALKED ACROSS THE LOUNGE. I JUST THOUGHT THAT'S WHAT OLD BIRDS' HOUSES DID.

Solution THE BRICK PIERS HOLDING UP THE BEARERS AND JOISTS UNDER THE FLOOR WERE ORIGINALLY LAID ON A LIME MORTAR BED. OVER TIME THE MORTAR HAS WORN SLIGHTLY OR THE PIERS HAVE SUNK, CREATING A GAP BETWEEN THE BEARER AND THE PIER. THAT GAP IS THE BOUNCE, AND THE BOUNCE WILL TRANSFER OVER TO THE CHINA CABINET, MAKING THE PLATES RATTLE.

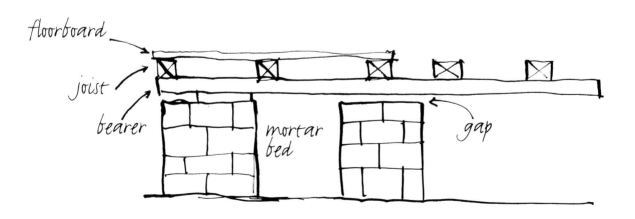

floorboard
joist
bearer
mortar bed
gap

YOU HAVE TO PACK THAT GAP. THAT MEANS...
YES, YOU HAVE TO GET UNDER THE HOUSE. TAKE
A DEEP BREATH AND TOUGHEN UP.

1 YOU CAN BUY LOAD-BEARING PLASTIC
WEDGES THAT WILL FILL THE GAP BETWEEN
THE PIER AND THE BEARER. DON'T OVERPACK
THE BEARER OR YOU'LL END UP WITH A HIGH
SPOT IN THE LOUNGE.

2 ALSO, IT'S POSSIBLE YOUR BEARERS OR JOISTS
AROUND THE PERIMETER OF THE ROOM WILL
SLOT INTO A CUTOUT IN THE BRICK WALL.
THERE IS USUALLY A GAP UNDERNEATH THE
BEARER OR JOIST IN THAT SLOT THAT NEEDS
PACKING. IF YOU PACK THE PIERS AND NOT THE
PERIMETER YOU'LL STILL HAVE THE BOUNCE.

3 GET SOMEONE IN THE ROOM TO BOUNCE UP
AND DOWN TO CHECK YOUR JOB.

THERE'S NOTHING MORE ROMANTIC THAN
SCREAMING AT THE MISSUS FROM UNDER THE
FLOOR OR, VICE VERSA, HAVING THE MISSUS
SCREAM AT YOU FROM UNDER THERE. AND ALL
THE PERSON ABOVE IS SAYING IS 'WHAT?'

Helpers

It's always good to have someone give you a hand when you're doing a bit of work around the house. Hold this, pass me that, get me a beer — that's why they invented first year apprentices. I've had a few apprentices over the years and they've all been terrific blokes and ended up great tradesmen. But it still doesn't stop you having a bit of fun.

'Right-o, mate, off you go for a smoko. Write this down — two pies, one with sauce, four sausage rolls, a black and white cake, one potato pie and a randy tart. Hurry up!'

'Right-o, mate, off to the hardware. Box of 3-inch nails — bullet heads — two hacksaw blades, a skirting board ladder and a long weight.'

It's very childish. The boys always get a good laugh 'cause the same thing happened to all of us, and when those apprentices finish their time they can't wait to get an apprentice and do the same.

Safety is always a big issue with apprentices. They're young and dumb and full of confidence...

We had a young bloke years ago who got his confidence up a bit early. Instead of getting a ladder to nail off a bit of timber that was a bit high, he did the full stretch with the nail gun on the tippy toes, and nailed his thumb straight through the first knuckle onto the stud work. He could've given Rudolf Nureyev a run for his money the way he was balancing on those toes of his.

Always get comfortable when you're doing work, and make sure your helper is comfy and takes the time to get the ladder or change position and doesn't rush — that way everyone can have a beer at the end of the day.

To save our little mate I popped him on my shoulders and one of the other boys cut out the bit of timber from the wall that his thumb was attached to, and we carted him off to hospital.

He was fairly embarrassed, walking up the hospital corridor with 200 mm of 4 X 2 in oregon attached to his thumb...

Job 2 ROTTEN JOIST

Problem IT'S ALMOST IMPOSSIBLE TO REPLACE THE WHOLE JOIST, BECAUSE YOU JUST CAN'T GET IT IN THERE AMONGST THE BEARERS AND PIERS AND OTHER JOISTS.

Solution THE GO IS TO PUT A BANDAID ON THE ROTTEN SECTION — THAT IS, TO NAIL A PIECE OF THE SAME MATERIAL WHERE THE ROTTEN SECTION IS AND MAKE SURE THAT PIECE SPANS BEYOND THE

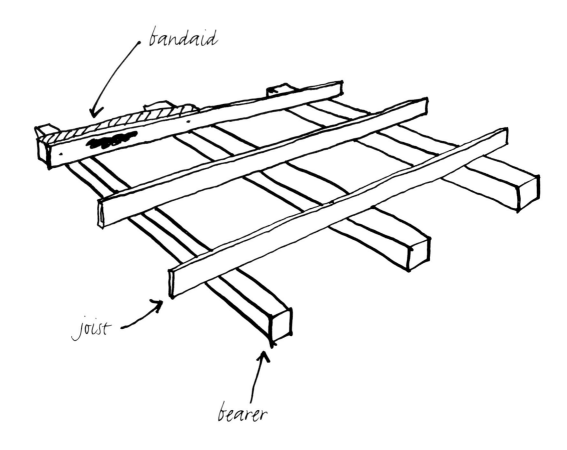

bandaid

joist

bearer

ROT AND INTO SOLID TIMBER. USUALLY A FLOOR JOIST IS 100 x 50 MM (4 x 2 IN) HARDWOOD.

AS LONG AS YOU SPAN FROM BEARER TO BEARER YOU'LL KEEP THE STRUCTURAL INTEGRITY OF THE FLOOR JOIST AND THERE'LL BE NO MORE FLEX IN THE FLOOR. REMEMBER, ALWAYS INVESTIGATE THE CAUSE OF THE ROTTEN JOIST AND FIX THAT PROBLEM TOO. IT'S PROBABLY TERMITES, OR DAMP OR DRY ROT.

DECK BOARDS

WHAT TYPE OF BOARD SHOULD YOU CHOOSE FOR THE DECK? BASICALLY THERE'RE TWO TYPES OF BOARD — HARDWOOD AND TREATED PINE.

IF YOU DON'T KNOW WHAT TREATED PINE LOOKS LIKE, GET A SAMPLE TO CHECK IT OUT. THEN TRY AND FIND AN OLD DECK TO HAVE A GANDER AT, BECAUSE I RECKON TREATED PINE DECKS DON'T AGE WELL AND LOOK PRETTY ORDINARY AFTER A FEW YEARS IF THEY'RE NOT MAINTAINED PROPERLY.

HARDWOOD MATURES WITH AGE AND GETS THAT GREY WHARF LOOK ABOUT IT. IF YOUR TIMBER IS A RICH RED, WITH THAT BEAUTIFUL HARDWOOD LOOK, IF LEFT IT WILL BECOME GREY WITHIN 12 MONTHS. YOU MUST KEEP THE DECK OIL UP TO IT EVERY SIX MONTHS. USE ONE WITH AN ULTRAVIOLET PROTECTANT IN IT AND SPLASH IT ON. BOTH HARDWOOD AND TREATED PINE DO A GREAT JOB IF MAINTAINED WELL.

ONE OTHER THING. SOME DECKING BOARDS HAVE A RIBBED FACE. THIS FACE IS DESIGNED TO GO ON THE UNDERSIDE OF THE BOARD TO ALLOW AIR FLOW BETWEEN THE BOARD AND THE JOIST. THIS PREVENTS THE BUILDUP OF MOISTURE, THEREBY REDUCING THE LIKELIHOOD OF THE TIMBER ROTTING.

SOME PEOPLE SAY IT'S FOR GRIP. THAT'S RUBBISH, AND WHEN THIS BOARD IS LAID RIBBED FACE UP, IT COLLECTS DIRT AND MOSS, AND BECOMES SLIPPERY AS MOISTURE IS RETAINED IN THE RIBS. I FIND THAT THE RIBS CAN SPLINTER AND BECOME DANGEROUS.

HAVE I TALKED YOU OUT OF IT YET? RIBS DOWN, SMOOTH UP.

23

Fair Dinkum Kev

There was this old bloke I used to work with. He loved his schooners, and telling a few 'porkies'. He drank a little too much, and he used to urinate outside the door of his jackaroo quarters. There was a dead patch of grass that would never grow.

We used to call him 'Fair Dinkum Kev' 'cause he used to tell a tall story or two, and all the way through each story we'd stand around him and say, 'Fair dinkum, Kev!'

We wouldn't let Kev drive 'cause he loved the schooners, so he used to ride an old pushbike with a clip around his pants, no gears, back peddle brakes. A 65-year-old bloke who drank himself to 100. He looked like the postie in The Sullivans.

Kev absolutely loved Goanna Oil — for everything from sore joints to lubing up the pushbike chain. Kev reckoned Goanna Oil was probably the best lubricant ever invented, and needless to say he had it smothered all over the old postie bike.

24

We all doubted Goanna Oil's properties so Kev, as true as he was standing there, told us a story...Fair dinkum, Kev...

He was riding home from the Top Pub down the Nielsen Road late the other night. He'd only had two schooners...'Fair dinkum, Kev!'...when an emu ran out in front of him. Not wanting to hurt the emu, Kev swerved to the left onto the gravel, through the guide posts, and off a steep embankment, flying through the air to the gully below. 'Fair dinkum, Kev!' Kev landed and was knocked out. The pushbike flew through the air and got stuck in a tree high above him. 'Fair dinkum, Kev!'

He woke about an hour later, dazed and confused, and walked the long way home.

The next morning Kev woke up feeling a lot better, took a leak outside his door, and started the long hike back to the crash site to retrieve the pushie.

He climbed down the embankment, got to the tree where the bike was — and you wouldn't believe it...the back wheel was still spinning!

'Fair dinkum, Kev!!!'

Job 3 CREAKING FLOORBOARD

Problem NOTHING MORE ANNOYING THAN SNEAKING IN LATE AT NIGHT AND HITTING THE OLD CREAKY FLOORBOARD AND GIVING THE GAME UP. AND EVERY DAY WHEN YOU HIT THAT SPOT...I MUST FIX THAT.

Solution YOU MUST UNDERSTAND THE CAUSE FIRST. WHEN TWO BOARDS ARE TIGHT TOGETHER AND HAVE LIFTED SLIGHTLY OFF THE JOIST, YOU STAND ON ONE, AND THE BOARD RUBS ON THE OTHER BOARD AS IT GOES DOWN UNDER YOUR WEIGHT AND CREAKS. SO THEREFORE THERE'S MOVEMENT, AND YOU HAVE TO SECURE THAT BOARD AND STOP IT FROM MOVING.

Carpet over floorboards

1 IF YOU HAVE NO PLANS FOR POLISHING THE FLOORBOARDS AND THERE'S CARPET, CAREFULLY LIFT THE CARPET.

2 USING A COUNTERSUNK SCREW HEAD, SCREW THE BOARDS DOWN WHERE IT CREAKS.

Polished floorboards

FOR A CREAKING POLISHED BOARD YOUR BEST BET IS TO GAIN ACCESS UNDER THE FLOOR.

1 FIND THE CREAKS UNDER THE FLOOR. THERE SHOULD BE A TINY GAP BETWEEN THE UNDERSIDE OF THE FLOORBOARD AND THE TOP OF THE JOIST.

2 HAVE SOME SMALL WOODEN WEDGES READY. SQUIRT WOOD GLUE ALL OVER EACH WEDGE AND IN THE GAP, AND TAP THEM IN. DON'T OVERTAP THE WEDGES AS THEY WILL CAUSE THE BOARD TO LIFT.

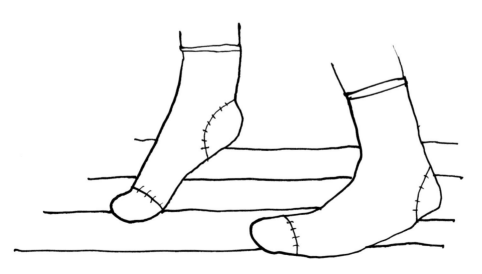

carpentry

Job 4 BROKEN FLOORBOARD

Problem THE HARDEST PART ABOUT FIXING A BUSTED OR ROTTEN FLOORBOARD IS MATCHING IT UP.

Solution

1 REMOVE THE ROTTEN FLOORBOARD AND TAKE A SAMPLE UP TO THE TIMBER YARD SO YOU CAN MATCH IT.

2 IF ALL ELSE FAILS, USE BOARDS FROM A ROOM WITH CARPET, IF YOU HAVE ONE. LIFT A CORNER OF THE CARPET AND PINCH A BOARD FROM THERE, AND REPLACE IT WITH ANY OLD BOARD. THE ONE IN THE ROOM WITH CARPET WILL ALWAYS MATCH YOUR ROTTEN ONE, AS THE BOARDS WOULD HAVE BEEN LAID AT THE SAME TIME, AS LONG AS THE HOUSE HASN'T BEEN RENOVATED SINCE THEN.

3 TO CUT THE BAD BOARD OUT YOU'LL NEED A CIRCULAR SAW. SET THE DEPTH OF THE CUT ON THE SAW TO 20 MM ($^3/_4$ IN), THE THICKNESS OF THE FLOORBOARD.

4 FIND THE NAILS IN THE BOARD. THESE SHOW YOU WHERE THE JOISTS ARE. YOU NEED TO CUT FROM JOIST TO JOIST SO THAT YOU CAN NAIL THE NEW BOARD IN. DRAW A SQUARE LINE AT EACH END OF THE CROOK BOARD — MAKE SURE EACH ONE IS HALFWAY ACROSS THE JOIST. THESE LINES ARE WHERE YOU CUT.

5 YOU MUST ALSO CUT DOWN THE LENGTH OF THE BOARD ON BOTH SIDES ABOUT 5–10 MM (1/4–1/2 IN) IN FROM THE EDGE. THIS WILL MAKE IT EASIER TO GET THE BOARD OUT.

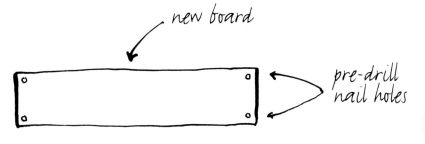

new board

pre-drill nail holes

6 THE CIRCULAR SAW WILL NOT MAKE IT THROUGH THE ENTIRE BOARD BECAUSE OF THE CURVE IN THE BLADE, SO A SHARP CHISEL IS THE GO, JUST TO FINISH THE CUT OFF AND CLEAN THINGS UP.

7 NOW JUST CUT A NEW PIECE OF BOARD THE SAME SIZE AS YOUR OPENING AND SLOT HER IN. REMEMBER TO PRE-DRILL THE ENDS OF THE FLOORBOARD SO THE NAILS WON'T SPLIT THE BOARD.

The structural cabinet

A great mate of mine is a doctor and a very good oncologist. I have great admiration for him and the work he does, but as a builder he's as handy as two away sick. I always say to him, 'stick to the stethoscope, or someone's gonna get hurt.' As usual he didn't listen, and I get the phone call Saturday morning. 'Mate, I've got a drama...I was ripping out the built-in cabinet and shelving that runs through the middle of the lounge — yep, you know the one. I decided to cut through the middle with a circular saw.'

There's his problem straightaway — he's got hold of a power saw. In his case this should be illegal. 'It looks like the ceiling dropped a bit and squashed the cabinet down, and now the saw is stuck in the cut I made.'

'Don't touch a thing, I'll come over so I can understand what you're talking about.'

The cabinet was made of a veneered ply, and was fairly large and solid. It went from floor to ceiling. He was right — the saw blade was stuck about three-quarters along his cut and no one was budging it.

'It must be under a load,' I told the Doc. 'Get me a ladder and I'll get up in the roof and see what's going on.' Then he started spruiking. 'Wait till you see what I've done up there!' I thought, 'shit! He's been up in the roof! Anything could have happened.'

Then he filled me in. About six months ago he noticed the roof was sagging a bit, so he got up in the roof space to find that the big bit of wood running across the wood coming down towards the gutter was broken (his words). In other words, the purlin which supported the roof rafters had snapped.

He had jacked it up somehow, and put struts and bracing to hold the sagging roof in pozzi. On the whole he'd done a good job — all the cuts were neat and it looked almost semi-professional. Except he'd run all the props onto one ceiling rafter, which is 100 x 50 mm (4 x 2 in) and designed to hold up plaster, not a roof. And directly underneath that rafter...the cabinet.

So at the end of the day the TV cabinet in the middle of the lounge was holding his roof up. No wonder the saw got stuck.

Nice one, Doc.

carpentry

Job 5 REPLACING SKIRTING BOARD

Problem YOUR SKIRTING BOARDS AREN'T LOOKING TOO FLASH. THEY'RE EITHER DAMAGED OR ROTTEN.

Solution IF YOU'RE USING SQUARE-EDGED SKIRTING THEN THE JOB IS FAIRLY SIMPLE — JUST A MATTER OF CUTTING IT TO LENGTH AND NAILING IT INTO YOUR STUD WALL. IF YOUR WALL IS MASONRY, THE SAME PRINCIPLE APPLIES. JUST USE GREEN PLUGS AND SCREWS, OR SPAGHETTI AND NAILS. SPAGHETTI IS THE SAME AS A GREEN PLUG BUT IT TAKES A NAIL INSTEAD OF A SCREW.

screw + green plug

FOR SQUARE-EDGED SKIRTING A BUTT JOINT IN THE CORNERS IS ACCEPTABLE. A BUTT JOINT IS JUST TWO PIECES OF TIMBER CUT SQUARE AND FIXED TOGETHER.

spaghetti + nail

IF YOUR SKIRTING HAS A PATTERNED PROFILE, SUCH AS BULL NOSE OR COLONIAL, THIS IS WHERE IT GETS FAIR DINKUM TO MEET THE TWO PIECES IN THE CORNER. YOU HAVE TO DO

32

WHAT'S CALLED A SCRIBE JOINT. THESE TAKE
A LOT OF PRACTICE AND IT WOULD PAY TO
BUY A LITTLE EXTRA SKIRTING TO HAVE A BIT
OF A GO BEFOREHAND TO PERFECT IT. IF YOU
CAN PULL THIS OFF YOU'RE GOING WELL.

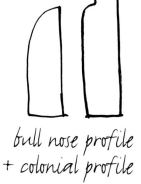

bull nose profile
+ colonial profile

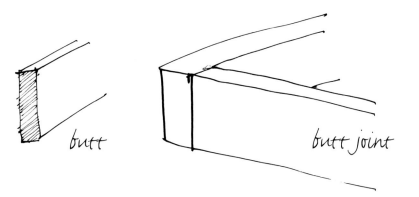

butt

butt joint

1 YOU HAVE TO CUT THE SKIRTING 45 DEGREES
ACROSS THE FACE OF THE TIMBER. THE CUT
WILL GIVE YOU AN EDGE WHICH REPRESENTS
YOUR SCRIBE CUT. THIS IS WHERE THE GOING
GETS TOUGH.

45-degree cut

2 USING A COPING SAW, FOLLOW THAT LINE.
ONCE YOU'VE CUT IT OUT, YOU WILL HAVE THE
SAME SHAPE AS THE SKIRTING FACE AND IT
WILL THEN FIT PERFECTLY WHEN YOU JOIN THE
INTERNAL CORNER.

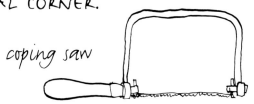

coping saw

scribe joint

carpentry

Job 6 SQUEAKING STAIR TREAD

Problem LIKE THE CREAKY FLOORBOARDS, YOU DON'T WANT THE CREAKY STAIRCASE LETTING EVERYONE KNOW WHAT TIME YOU'RE GETTING IN.

Solution IF YOUR STAIRS ARE SQUEAKING IT MEANS THERE IS MOVEMENT IN ONE OF YOUR TREADS. JUMP IN UNDER YOUR STAIRS — MOST SETS HAVE ACCESS.

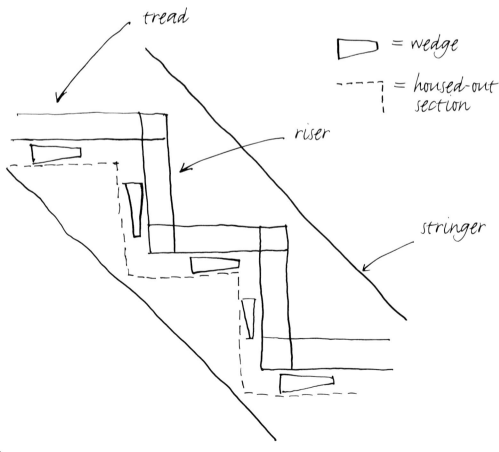

tread

riser

stringer

▱ = wedge

- - -┐ = housed-out
  ╎   section

1 UNDERNEATH YOU WILL SEE YOUR TWO STRINGERS, WHICH ARE THE LONG TIMBERS RUNNING DOWN EITHER SIDE OF THE STAIRS.

2 YOU'LL ALSO SEE HOUSED-OUT SECTIONS IN THE SHAPE OF STAIRS ON EACH STRINGER. THE RISERS AND TREADS SIT IN THESE HOUSE-OUTS, WITH TIMBER WEDGES KEEPING THEM IN PLACE.

3 SQUIRT SOME WOODWORK GLUE AROUND THE LOOSE WEDGE AND TAP IT IN UNTIL IT'S TIGHT. THIS WILL TIGHTEN UP THE TREAD AND KNOCK OFF THE SQUEAK.

First day

During my travels around Australia I had a bit of a dream of becoming a shipwright. For those of you who don't know, a shipwright is a boat builder. I used to picture myself shaving a bit of timber down on the shore of a Greek island, drinking ouzo for smoko and surrounded by good sorts. My missus still won't let me go to Greece.

Reality hit me when I got up one morning at 6 am and hooked it off through Fremantle, WA, knocking on doors looking for a shipwright's job. Being a carpenter I had the tools and the skills, but lacked a bit on the technical side, but being young and not worrying about too much, I was telling all my prospective employers I was a 10-year shipwright veteran, did my time at Halverson in Bobbin Head, NSW, and was apprenticed to Billy Campbell (Billy was a plumber mate of mine back home).

I'd tell the boss that Billy had died six months prior in a boat winch accident so he couldn't be contacted. Of course Billy was as healthy as, probably due to the fact that there're aren't too many boat winches in the plumbing game.

36

'Oh, shit, yes, mate, worked on Riverovas, Bertrams, the lot.'

Eventually someone fell for the story and at 3 pm that day, I was a shipwright, due to start at 6 am the next day.

I arrived in the workshop keen as a bean. I was introduced to all the blokes and then the boss gave me the world's biggest wrap, telling the boys where I'd worked. I'm sitting there thinking, 'It's all downhill from here.'

I may have dug myself into a hole, but I was planning on getting out of it. I just wasn't sure how!

The boss began assigning jobs to the boys. 'Johnno and Pete, into the freezer compartments. Mick and Heff, start setting out the deck, and Steve, you and Scotty fit out the wheelhouse.' The boss gave me the plans and on the way to the wheelhouse (which was the size of a one-bedroom flat) I had a bit of a squizz at them. They looked like the plans of the cockpit on the Concorde. I thought to myself, 'I'm in all sorts here.'

I would eventually have worked it out, but the big problem was I didn't have a spare week. I had about 30 seconds climbing up the ladder into the wheelhouse to come up with a plan.

Steve was a big bloke and he wasn't too impressed with the way the boss was wrapping me before I'd struck a blow. Steve was a sceptic, and his intuition was spot on. We were now in the wheelhouse, the plans rolled out and pinned on the wall.

Steve and I are both looking at them, he's testing me, waiting for me to speak. When no plan jumped out at me, I panicked.

It was almost like Bobby from The Practice was screaming at me with the full finger point until I broke down. 'Steve, this is my first day as a shipwright. I have no idea what I'm doing. If you could carry me for a week, I'm sure I'll be fine.' I said this very quickly, the full confession.

Pause. Silence.

Steve looked at me in horror. 'You're f****** shittin' me!'

'I wish I was shittin' ya.'

Luckily Steve saw the funny side and began to laugh. 'How the f*** did you get this far...'

Steve and I worked together for 18 months and became good mates. He taught me heaps.

39

carpentry

Job 7 INSTALLING INSULATION

Problem A LOT OF OLD HOMES DON'T HAVE ANY INSULATION IN THE CEILING. WE KNOW INSULATION BY THE GENERIC NAME OF PINK BATTS. YOU CAN REALLY COOL DOWN YOUR HOUSE BY PUTTING THEM IN, AND YOU CAN SAVE MONEY BY DOING IT YOURSELF. CHECK WITH YOUR SUPPLIER ON THE RATING OF YOUR BATTS, AS SOME ARE MORE EFFECTIVE THAN OTHERS. THE MORE EFFECTIVE THEY ARE, THE MORE EXPENSIVE THEY'LL BE.

Solution FIRSTLY, PICK A FAIRLY COOL DAY 'CAUSE THIS IS A NASTY JOB. THE CEILING SPACE IS HOT AND DUSTY, AND PUTTING THE BATTS IN IS VERY UNCOMFORTABLE. THE FIBRES FROM THE BATTS STICK TO YOUR SWEAT AND MAKE YOU SCRATCH LIKE A ONE-ARMED CABBIE WITH CRABS.

TO AVOID THIS, GET SOME PAPER OVERALLS, GLOVES, EYE PROTECTION AND A DUST MASK. THE MOST IMPORTANT PART OF THIS PROCEDURE IS TO

40

TAPE UP THE GAPS. TAPE THE
OVERALLS TO YOUR GLOVES AND
SOCKS, AND TRY AND GET SOME
UNDER YOUR CHIN. NOW YOU'RE
READY TO GET THE BATTS UP THROUGH
THE MANHOLE AND LAY THEM OUT.

2 LAY THE BATTS IN BETWEEN THE CEILING
RAFTERS SO THEY'RE TOUCHING THE CEILING.
IF THERE ARE ANY PIPES OR TIMBERS IN THE
WAY, JUST CUT THE BATTS WITH A SHARP
STANLEY KNIFE AND POKE OFFCUTS IN
THE GAPS.

carpentry

Job 8 OUT OF SQUARE DOOR JAMB

Problem YOU'RE TRYING TO HANG A NEW DOOR, AND THE DOOR JAMB IS OUT OF SQUARE.

Solution IF YOU'RE GOING TO HAVE A CRACK AT THIS JOB, IT'S GOING TO BE VERY DIFFICULT. THIS METHOD IS ONLY SUITABLE FOR A SOLID DOOR.

1 A LITTLE TRICK SO YOU DON'T STUFF UP YOUR BRAND NEW DOOR. GO DOWN TO THE HARDWARE STORE AND ASK THEM FOR A COVER SHEET FROM THEIR PLY STOCK. WHEN THEY GET A PLY OR USUALLY ANY SHEET DELIVERY, EACH BUNDLE HAS A 3 MM ($1/10$ IN) COVER SHEET TOP AND BOTTOM. YOU CAN ALMOST ALWAYS GET THEM FOR FREE.

2 CUT THE COVER SHEET ABOUT 100 MM (4 IN) BIGGER THAN YOUR DOOR OPENING.

3 GET SOMEONE TO HOLD THAT UP AGAINST THE DOOR OPENING AND MARK IT OUT FROM THE OTHER SIDE — MAKE THIS MARK ABOUT 5 MM ($1/4$ IN) BIGGER THAN THE DOORWAY.

4 KEEP TRIMMING THE COVER SHEET UNTIL IT FITS PERFECTLY IN YOUR DOORWAY. USE A STANLEY KNIFE FOR GYPROCK OR A PLANE FOR TIMBER. NOW LAY YOUR TEMPLATE ON THE DOOR, AND TRACE AROUND IT WITH A PENCIL. CUT IT OUT WITH A CIRCULAR SAW OR A HANDSAW. IF THE TEMPLATE'S RIGHT, THE DOOR'S RIGHT.

carpentry

Job 9 PROBLEMS WITH A SLIDING DOOR

Problem IF THE SLIDING DOOR IS FAIRLY OLD, IT'S PROBABLY THE CASE THAT THE NYLON WHEEL OF THE ROLLER HAS WORN OUT AND NEEDS TO BE REPLACED.

Solution SLIDING DOORS HAVE TWO ROLLERS ON THE UNDERSIDE OF THE DOOR. THESE CAN BE ADJUSTED TO RAISE OR LOWER THE DOOR. AT EACH EDGE DOWN THE BOTTOM OF AN ALUMINIUM SLIDING DOOR THERE'S A HOLE WITH AN ADJUSTMENT SCREW. THIS WILL RAISE OR LOWER THE ROLLER AND DO THE SAME TO THE DOOR. YOU CAN LINE UP YOUR LOCK DOING THIS OR JUST SQUARE UP THE DOOR.

1 REMOVE THE DOOR BY LIFTING IT UP AND PULLING IT OUT AT THE BOTTOM. THE DOOR WILL COME OUT AT THE BOTTOM TRACK AND THEN DROP DOWN OUT OF THE TOP TRACK.

door frame

roller

wheel

44

2 THE ROLLERS ARE IN A CHANNEL AT THE BOTTOM OF THE DOOR AND CAN USUALLY JUST BE LEVERED OUT WITH A SCREWDRIVER. THERE ARE MANY TYPES OF ROLLERS, SO TAKE THEM WITH YOU TO THE HARDWARE SO YOU CAN BUY THE RIGHT REPLACEMENT ROLLERS.

3 WACK THE NEW ONES IN, THEN PUT THE DOOR BACK IN. PUT THE TOP INTO THE TOP TRACK FIRST, THEN DO THE BOTTOM.

4 ADJUST TO SUIT YOUR LOCK.

changing the prop

Once I'd had 18 months' experience working as a shipwright, the BS came a little easier. I knew some terms — I even sounded like I knew what I was talking about — so in my travels around Australia I was always looking for work on boats.

I arrived in a small coastal town in northern Western Australia. The resort there had two charter boats, and they were looking for a resort carpenter and a shipwright to maintain the boats.

I couldn't believe it. I started spruiking. In the end I was a cold schooner and they were dying of thirst in the desert. They had to have me.

Frank, the guy who owned the small resort, was also one of the skippers. He was MAD. He'd been around boats all his life. If it had the ocean or boats attached to it, he'd done it.

Frightened of nothing, he was the best fisherman and snorkler I've ever seen.

One day Frank, myself and two other blokes were working on one of the boats, doing a bit of maintenance. Frank says, 'We're going out to sea to pump the bilge.' We were based in Exmouth Gulf. Best fishing I've ever seen and the most sharks I've ever seen. Nine times out of ten, wherever you were in the Gulf fishing, you'd have to move after a short while 'cause sharks were taking your fish on the way up.

Frank gets us about three miles out, shuts down the motor and says, 'What about we change the prop. I've got the new one here. We'll all wack on some fins, tread water and change the prop. It'll only take an hour.' An hour! Treading water dressed like a seal, perfect. I wished I'd rung my Mum that morning.

'Frank, what's wrong with changing the prop back at the mooring?'

47

Frank laughs and says, 'What are you — a poofter?'

'No, no, there's nothing wrong with out here. It's just we might drop it.' I was looking for excuses to restore my manhood.

'We're going to tie a rope around it. What are you, a poofter and stupid?'

'Right-o, right-o, give us the fins.'

In the water I go. Along with everyone else, I'm under the boat trying to get the old prop off, using a dolly and a lump hammer to knock the pin out. After half an hour of treading water, I'd re-run Jaws 1, 2 and 3 through my head, and was hoping that Frank was the first to go — firstly 'cause he called me a poofter and secondly so I could say, 'I told you so!' as he was eaten alive.

With the old prop off and the new one dangling off two ropes in the

48

water, Frank
made the call.
Someone had to get
on board and adjust
the ropes to line the prop up.

Well, with my huge fins on, I was like Flipper flying
out of the water towards the dolphin trainer
hanging out the fresh sardine. I think I landed on
the deck of the boat in one motion, at the same
time calling, 'I'll do it!'

Once the new prop was on and we were motoring
home, no one was any the wiser that the first thing
I had to do was change me speedos (not literally!!!!).

49

Job 10 DOOR NOT CLOSING

Problem IT'S PRETTY RARE TO FIND A HOUSE, ESPECIALLY ONE OF AGE, THAT HAS EVERY DOOR IN THE HOUSE CLOSING PERFECTLY WITHOUT CATCHING ON THE JAMB. WHEN I WAS GROWING UP WE HAD ABOUT FIVE DOORS THAT GRABBED OR CLIPPED THE JAMB, OR JUST DIDN'T CLOSE. INSTEAD OF FIXING THEM, WE ADAPTED TO THE SITUATION. GRAB THE HANDLE, LIFT AND PULL TO THE LEFT AND TURN THE KEY AT SAME TIME — PRESTO, TOO EASY.

Solution THERE ARE A FEW CAUSES. POORLY FITTED, LOOSE HINGES, SWELLING, AND CONTINUOUS PAINTING OVER THE YEARS OF THE DOOR AND JAMB CAN CAUSE THE DOOR TO CATCH.

Loose hinges

HOPEFULLY, IT'S THE HINGES. THIS IS THE EASIEST TO FIX. USUALLY THE TOP HINGE HAS LOOSENED ON THE DOOR OR THE JAMB UNDER THE WEIGHT AND MOVEMENT. TRY TIGHTENING THE SCREWS.

1 You'll probably find the holes have been stripped, so take out one screw at a time and slot in one or two matches (depending on the size of the hole).

2 Snap off the excess and replace the screw. This will tighten the hinges, pull the door back up and create the gap required for the door to close smoothly.

Swollen or overpainted door

If the door is swollen or overpainted, then you'll have to wack the bag on and plane the door off. Planing timber is full-on tradesman stuff, so the family will be impressed. Make sure you look the part.

1 Before you remove the door, use a pencil to mark out the area and depth of the sections to be planed.

2 Remove the door and stand it up on the ground in a door clamp (just a bit of 100 x 50 mm or 4 x 2 in timber with a cut-out

wedge
door clamp

SLOT THAT'S A BIT BIGGER THAN THE WIDTH OF THE DOOR). SLOT A WEDGE IN WITH THE DOOR TO KEEP IT STABLE. THE WEDGE CAN BE WOOD, OR EVEN A CHISEL.

3 REMOVE THE LATCH SO THE PLANE DOESN'T GET DAMAGED, AND PLANE AWAY. WHEN YOU'RE HAPPY, PUT THE DOOR BACK ON.

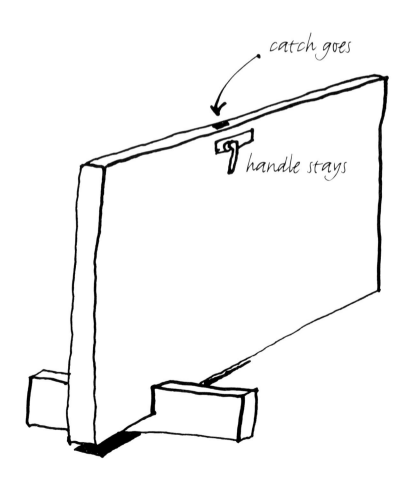

catch goes

handle stays

Bernie

I've got a mate I have a beer with most nights. Top bloke, but fair dinkum hopeless. Hopeless at everything he touches. He's good at business and making a quid, but apart from that he's as useful as two away sick.

About once a month Bernie comes in the pub, rubbing his hand from his forehead up through his hair, whilst blowing out the mouth with his eyes wide open and shaking his head, saying, 'You'll never guess what happened to me.'

All the boys say, 'Oh McGoo, you've done it again.' It's a bit of a ritual with Bernie.

He's tried to fix something around the house and killed the cat. It's always the most unlikely situation and unbelievable outcome, but that's our mate McGoo. And it makes for a bloody good laugh.

Let me say that Bernie was given a few gifts. He's a terrific style of a

53

bloke and the girls always go crazy over him. And he's a terrific sportsman, being a first grader in a few sports. One of those blokes — good lookin' and good at everything.

Which makes it all the funnier that he's a complete and utter knucklehead.

The other thing about Bernie — he's a great sport and cops the bagging on the chin and has a laugh at himself.

So later on, when I tell you a bit of a story about Bernie, you've got a bit of history about me ol' mate McGoo.

Job 11 STIFF LOCK OR KEY HOLE

Problem THE FIRST THING EVERYONE THINKS OF FOR A STIFF LOCK OR KEY HOLE IS **WD 40**, SINGER MACHINE OIL OR GREASE. THESE GUYS MAY WORK FOR A SHORT TIME BUT NOT FOR LONG. THEY ATTRACT DUST AND DIRT, AND WILL CLOG UP THE MECHANISM AND MAKE IT STIFF AGAIN.

Solution WHAT YOU NEED IS SOME GRAPHITE. YOU CAN BUY IT IN A FINE POWDER FORM. IT COMES IN A PLASTIC CONTAINER WITH A POINTY NOZZLE.

1 SQUIRT IT ON THE KEY AS WELL AS INTO THE KEY HOLE.

2 FOR A DEADLOCK OR DOOR HANDLE YOU MAY HAVE TO PULL THE LOCK OR HANDLE OFF AND SQUIRT THE GRAPHITE INTO THE LOCK.

3 THE LATCH ON THE EDGE OF THE DOOR IS A SEPARATE UNIT TO THE HANDLE. SQUIRT IT WITH GRAPHITE AS WELL SO THE WHOLE ACTION CAN MOVE SMOOTHLY.

Job 12 WINDOW LOCKS

Problem IF YOU DON'T HAVE WINDOW LOCKS, INSURANCE COMPANIES WON'T HAVE A BAR OF YOU MOST OF THE TIME. IT'S A GOOD IDEA TO HAVE THEM ANYWAY FOR SECURITY, AND YOU CAN LEAVE THE WINDOW OPEN A DASH FOR AIR FLOW AND STILL BE SECURE.

Solution THERE'S A HEAP OF LOCKS ON THE MARKET AND JUST AS MANY DIFFERENT TYPES OF WINDOWS, SO THERE'S NO POINT EXPLAINING HOW TO FIT THEM. THE MANUFACTURER'S INSTRUCTIONS SHOULD HELP THERE. BUT HERE ARE A FEW TIPS TO MAKE LIFE EASIER.

I MAKE SURE YOU GET ALL YOUR LOCKS KEYED ALIKE. THAT WAY ONE KEY FITS ALL. IF YOU'RE BUYING THEM AT THE HARDWARE, THEY HAVE A KEY CODE — USUALLY FIVE NUMBERS. JUST MATCH THEM UP FOR KEYED-ALIKE LOCKS.

2 THE LOCKS COME WITH A SET OF PHILLIPS-HEAD SCREWS AND A SET OF NO-RETURN SCREWS. IF YOU'RE RENTING AND WANT TO TAKE THE LOCKS WITH YOU WHEN YOU MOVE OUT, DON'T USE THE NO-RETURN SCREWS. THEY DO EXACTLY THAT — NO-RETURN, SO YOU CAN'T UNSCREW THEM.

3 FIT THE LOCKS WITH THE WINDOW IN THE CLOSED POSITION. LOCK THE TWO PARTS OF THE LOCK TOGETHER. THEN FIX IT TO THE WINDOW.

carpentry

Job 13 WINDOW WON'T OPEN

Problem Just about every old house has a window or two that won't open. And when you ask the owners about opening a window to let some air in, they say that the window has never opened. That's when I say, 'Get out of the way, ya dopes. Give us two minutes.'

Solution There're really only three reasons a window won't open — it's painted shut, it's swollen up or it's been nailed shut. If you find a fourth one, don't write me a letter.

Nailed shut

1 If it's nailed shut, obviously find the nails and dig out a bit of the timber around the heads to expose them.

2 Pull out the nails with pliers or pinchers.

3 Putty up the holes, then paint.

58

Painted shut

1 IF THE WINDOW IS PAINTED SHUT, GET YOURSELF A STANLEY KNIFE AND CAREFULLY CUT THE PAINT IN THE CORNER OF THE STOP BEAD (THE SMALL BEADING THAT HOLDS THE WINDOW IN) AND SASH.

2 USING A BLOCK OF TIMBER AND A HAMMER, PLACE THE TIMBER ON THE WINDOW FRAME AND VERY GENTLY GO AROUND AND TAP THE FRAME OF THE WINDOW. THEN JEMMY THE WINDOW UP.

Swollen shut

1 IF THE WINDOW IS SWOLLEN, IT NEEDS TO COME OUT. REMOVE THE STOP BEADS. YOU'LL BE ABLE TO POP THE WINDOW OUT WITH THE SASH CORDS STILL ATTACHED. IF YOU BREAK A STOP BEAD, JUST BUY SOME MORE. CHEAP AS CHIPS.

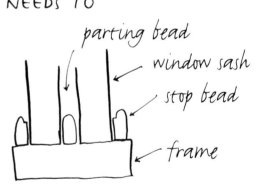

parting bead
window sash
stop bead
frame

2 RUN A PLANE AND A BIT OF SANDPAPER UP THE SIDES AND CLEAN UP THE OFFENDING EDGES.

3 POP THE WINDOW BACK IN AND MAKE SURE SHE GOES UP AND DOWN NICELY.

4 REPLACE THE STOP BEADS.

Job 14 BROKEN FLYSCREEN

Problem IT'S NORMALLY THE KIDDIES WHO DAMAGE THE FLYSCREENS BY POKING THEIR HANDS THROUGH. THEN YOU'VE GOT TO SIT THERE WATCHING THE TELLY, WITH THE CHEESE AND CRACKERS, NUTS, THE COLD BEER AND THE MORTEIN. THERE'S NOTHING WORSE THAN FLIES IN THE HOUSE.

Solution GET UP OFF THE COUCH. IT'LL TAKE YOU ONE AD BREAK TO FIX IT.

1 POP THE FLYSCREEN OUT AND LAY IT ON A TABLE. ON THE INSIDE OF THE FRAME IS A LITTLE REBATE. THE SCREEN IS HELD IN THERE WITH A SMALL RUBBER HOSE. FIND THE JOIN IN THE HOSE AND GET ONE END OUT WITH A SCREWDRIVER. GET A HOLD OF THE END AND PULL OUT THE LOT.

2 LAY THE NEW SCREEN OVER THE FRAME, ALLOWING ABOUT 50 MM (2 IN) EXTRA ALL THE WAY AROUND. START WITH ONE SIDE AND POKE THE HOSE INTO THE REBATE.

THIS WILL LOCK THE SCREEN INTO THE REBATE. TO MAKE LIFE EASY YOU CAN BUY A SPECIAL WHEEL TO DO THIS.

3 DON'T TENSION YOUR SCREEN TOO MUCH AS IT'LL BOW IN YOUR FRAME. IF YOU'RE LEFT WITH A CREASE, JUST PULL IT OUT AND START AGAIN.

4 NOW TRIM OFF THE EXCESS WITH A STANLEY KNIFE. BACK TO THE TELLY.

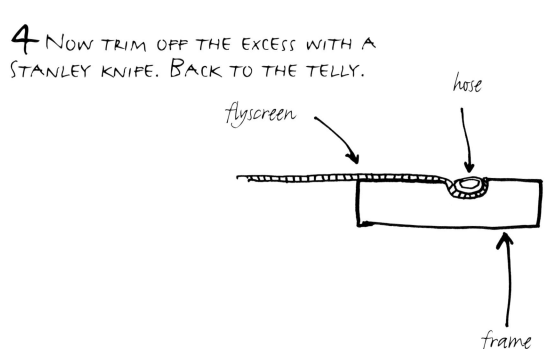

flyscreen

hose

frame

Bernie's honeymoon 1

Me old mate Bernie got married a few years ago. And he thought he'd do something different for his honeymoon. Most blokes get the hotel room at some fancy joint and don't leave it for a few days, and when they do they have to slip back up a few times a day with the new bride.

Not Bernie — he's gonna get a houseboat up north and cruise around Myall Lakes, 'cause he did that with his Mum and Dad 20 years ago and it was sensational. 'And it'll be so romantic and the bride is going to love it when I surprise her.' The Table of Knowledge (me and my mates when we're having a drink at the pub) all looked at Bernie. 'Surprise her? Bernie, we all agree that's not a good idea.'

'No probs, she'll love it. We'll fish and cruise and it'll be great.'

Under their breath, everyone said, 'Oh, McGoo, you've done it again.'

Anyway, Bernie went under the hammer, sold to the bird in white. A great night had by everyone. Off they go to the honeymoon.

About a week later Bernie walked into the pub with his usual look of misfortune. He's always very serious when he says, 'You'll never guess what happened to me.'

The Table broke up. 'What's happened, McGoo?'

Here's the story. It's a corker.

Bernie arrived at Myall Lakes to pick up his houseboat, the one in the brochure — rooftop deck, three bedrooms, great long bar, telly, the works. He couldn't believe how cheap it was. Except the one he booked wasn't the one in the brochure.

'That's top of the range,' the bloke laughed at him. 'That's worth five times what you paid.'

Basically, Bernie had booked himself and the new bride a 20-foot floating Millard caravan. Bernie explained, 'It was a shit box.' The bride was in tears. To save the day he gets out the gold credit card and upgrades to a middle of the range houseboat which the bride liked. Disaster averted.

You pick up these boats up the river, a fair hike from Myall Lakes. As it turns out, when you're going about four or five knots, it's about five hours. But Bernie was determined to get to that little cove where he and Mum and Dad stayed in 1975, and nothing was going to stop him.

Off they go at four knots up the river. It's about 10 am by this stage. No time to stop for funny business or food. Must press on and get to the Lakes. A great river with thick bush on both sides. Bernie was on a mission.

After belting along at a cracking four knots for four hours, the bride was getting restless and wanted a few drinks and a bit of action — the standard honeymoon. So Bernie backed the throttle off, went downstairs, got himself a cold one and mixed the bride up a nice cold housewife's heroin (gin and tonic). Off they go cruising, drinks in hand, life's good.

After another four hours (eight in total), the bride's in tears. Bernie can't understand where the Lakes are and darkness is setting in. All of a sudden he spots them. (The Table of Knowledge, all at once, said, 'The Lakes!')

No, the wharf where he'd hired the houseboat. When Bernie went down to mix the drinks, the houseboat did a 180-degree spin, so when he got back up to the wheel he was facing back up the river. He was only 15 minutes from the Lakes but motored the four hours back to the wharf. They tied up and spent the first night there and had a go at first light.

Oh, McGoo...

In part 2, later on, it gets worse.

Job 15 BUILDING SHELVING

Problem THE MISSUS IS AT YOU TO PUT SOME SHELVES UP IN THE HOUSE.

Solution YOU CAN DO THIS A NUMBER OF WAYS.

Basic shelf bracket

THESE ARE AVAILABLE IN ALL HARDWARE STORES... IF YOU CAN GET SOME BASTARD TO SERVE YOU.

basic shelf bracket

Ready-made unit

THESE ARE ADJUSTABLE AND AVAILABLE IN MOST HARDWARE STORES.

ready-made unit

Rough and ready

More shelves needed for the shed? This is the method I use all the time for some quick shelving.

1 Simply screw or nail a piece of 75 x 50 mm (3 x 2 in) timber nice and level to the wall, the same length as the shelf.

2 Make sure it's nice and solid, then screw down into the top of your 75 x 50 mm (3 x 2 in) a piece of 190 x 19 mm ($7^1/2$ x $^3/4$ in) timber to act as the shelf. If you need lots of shelving, buy a sheet of ply, get the timber yard to rip it down to 200 mm (8 in) strips and then cut it yourself to suit your shelving.

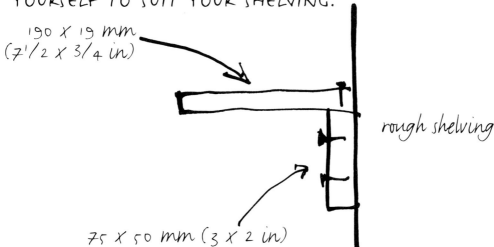

190 x 19 mm ($7^1/2$ x $3/4$ in)

rough shelving

75 x 50 mm (3 x 2 in)

Job 16 HANGING A PICTURE

Problem YOU NEED TO PUT A FASTENER ON THE WALL SO YOU CAN HANG A PICTURE...WITHOUT IT FALLING OFF A DAY LATER.

Solution THIS DEPENDS ON WHAT YOU'RE HANGING THE PICTURE ON.

Brick wall

AGAIN, DEPENDS ON THE WEIGHT OF THE PICTURE. FOR A SMALL PICTURE YOU'LL NEED AN IMPACT DRILL — THAT'S ONE WITH A HAMMER ACTION ON IT SO IT CAN DRILL THROUGH BRICKS.

1 USING A 6 MM (¼ IN) MASONRY DRILL BIT, DRILL A HOLE ABOUT 50 MM (2 IN) DEEP INTO YOUR BRICKWORK.

2 WALL PLUGS ARE AVAILABLE AT EVERY HARDWARE STORE. THEY'RE COLOUR CODED ACCORDING TO THEIR SIZE, SO 6 MM (¼ IN) IS A GREEN PLUG. TAP THE GREEN PLUG INTO YOUR HOLE UNTIL IT'S FLUSH WITH THE WALL.

screw + plug

68

3 EACH PLUG SUITS A CERTAIN SCREW SIZE —
JUST CHECK THE PACKET. ONCE YOU HAVE THE
RIGHT SCREW, ABOUT 50 MM (2 IN) LONG
AND 6 GAUGE, SCREW IT IN. LEAVE ABOUT
10 MM (1/2 IN) STICKING OUT OF THE PLUG
AND HANG YOUR PICTURE.

FOR BIGGER PICTURES YOU CAN GO UP THE
VARIOUS SIZES OF PLUGS AND SCREWS, OR GO
THE FULL HOG AND BUY A DYNA BOLT WITH A
CUP HOOK. SAME PRINCIPLE AS THE PLUG AND
SCREW. THERE ARE VARIOUS SIZES OF DYNA
BOLT AVAILABLE, DEPENDING ON THE SIZE OF
YOUR PICASSO.

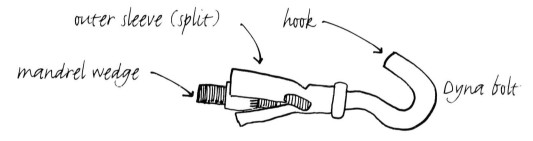

outer sleeve (split)   hook

mandrel wedge

Dyna bolt

1 DRILL THE HOLE TO SUIT THE SIZE OF THE
DYNA BOLT.

2 TAP THE BOLT STRAIGHT IN THE HOLE AND
TIGHTEN IT. THE OUTSIDE SLEEVE ON THE
DYNA BOLT SPREADS AND THE BOLT TIGHTENS
ON ITSELF.

carpentry

Timber wall

IT'S ALWAYS A BONUS IF YOU CAN FIND THE STRUCTURAL TIMBER IN THE WALL. ALLOW THE THICKNESS OF THE LINING BOARD (USUALLY EITHER 6 MM OR 1/4 IN FOR FIBRO OR 10 MM OR 1/2 IN FOR GYPROCK), ABOUT 30 MM (1 IN) PENETRATION INTO THE STUD WORK AND 10 MM (1/2 IN) PROUD TO HANG THE PICTURE.

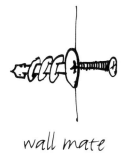

wall mate

YOU CANNOT PUT A SCREW STRAIGHT INTO PLASTERBOARD — IT WON'T HOLD THE SKIN OF A CUSTARD. YOU MUST FIND THE SOLID TIMBER BEHIND FOR STRENGTH. IF THAT'S IMPOSSIBLE, THERE'RE A FEW THINGS ON THE MARKET FOR GOING INTO THE PLASTERBOARD. TRY A WALL MATE OR A TOGGLE.

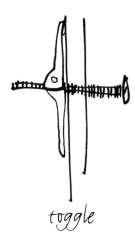

toggle

IF YOU'RE HANGING A VERY HEAVY PICTURE ONTO A PLASTERBOARD WALL, TRY TO FIND A STUD. KNOCK ALONG THE WALL WITH YOUR KNUCKLE, LISTENING FOR A CHANGE IN TONE. THE HOLLOW-SOUNDING BITS DON'T HAVE A STUD BEHIND THEM, SO LISTEN FOR A 'SOLID' SOUND.

70

My perfect day

It's not often you get a perfect day. I don't mean good weather, or your team won the grand final. I mean the bloody perfect day.

I woke at about 6.30 am. Good night's sleep, felt great, woke the minister for war and the three kids at 7. They were also in great moods. I thought, 'That's strange.' But anyway, 'Everybody, let's go.' Off to our usual Sunday morning at the beach — about an 8 am arrival.

It goes without saying the perfect day didn't have a cloud in the sky. Outside temp 32°, water temp about 21°, medium swell, easy-rolling, body-bash waves. Probably, in my view, about as perfect as beach conditions get.

We all had a great morning and around 11.30 we packed up and headed home. All the kids were very tired. They stripped off and had showers, then wandered off for an afternoon sleep. Suddenly I remembered I'd done a freebie for a mate of mine and he'd given me a case of Crownies and a bag of king prawns that I'd had on ice since the day before. It took me about 10 minutes to peel the monster prawns and 'cause my day was going so good I thought I'd treat myself and take the 'trails out. Big bowl of kingies, Thousand Island sauce and freezing cold Crownie in my favourite stubby holder. Shit, the wheels are gonna fall off the wagon shortly.

I set up all my gear on the coffee table in front of the telly — prawns, beer, sauce. Then my wife walked in, looked at the prawns — here we go. Then she says, 'I don't feel like a prawn. I'm gonna have a lie down with the kids. Do you mind?'

'Do I mind?...Are you out of your mind?' I thought. 'No, no, you go for it, darling.'

My gear is ready. I'm by myself. I flick the telly on. Could this be possible, it can't be, it is...it's the opening scene to Where Eagles Dare.

Everyone was asleep. The beach. The beer. The prawns. The movie.

As far as days go, in my mind I'd ridden a Melbourne Cup winner, kicked the winning goal against the All Blacks and received my Kangaroo Jersey and Baggy Green all in the one day.

As the credits rolled up on Where Eagles Dare, I was on my last prawn and just finishing off Crownie no. 6 when the three kids and the boss wandered out from their bedrooms rubbing their eyes.

Some unknown force kept those four asleep until the last prawn went down and until Richard Burton threw the baddie out of the plane. Whoever you are, I thank you.

The perfect day.

carpentry

Job 17   SWOLLEN KITCHEN CABINET

Problem YOU'RE IN A BIT OF STRIFE HERE. MOST KITCHENS THESE DAYS ARE MADE OF CHIPBOARD. WHEN CHIPBOARD GETS WET, IT SWELLS UP HORRIBLY AND STARTS TO FALL APART. AND REALLY, THERE'S NOTHING TO BE DONE ABOUT IT.

Solution IF IT'S A DOOR YOU'RE SWEET. JUST TAKE THE DOOR OFF AT THE HINGE, WHIP DOWN TO THE LOCAL KITCHEN MANUFACTURER AND GET THEM TO KNOCK YOU UP A NEW ONE.

IF IT'S IN THE CABINETS YOU'RE IN TROUBLE. YOU MAY BE ABLE TO LIFT THE BENCH TOP AND, BECAUSE MOST KITCHENS ARE MODULAR — THAT IS, EACH CABINET IS A SEPARATE UNIT — YOU COULD PULL THAT CABINET OUT AND GET THE KITCHEN GUY TO BUILD YOU A NEW ONE.

BUT BECAUSE MOST SWOLLEN CABINETS ARE AROUND THE SINK YOU'VE GOT THE SINK AND

PLUMBING TO CONTEND WITH, SO YOU'RE
BETTER OFF WITH AN EXPERT FOR THAT ONE.

SO IT DOESN'T HAPPEN AGAIN, WORK OUT
WHERE THE WATER'S COMING FROM AND CALL
THE PLUMBER. THE FOLLOWING ARE SOME
COMMON CAUSES.

1 THE TRAP UNDER THE SINK IS LEAKING.

2 THE SEAL AROUND THE TOP OF THE SINK
HAS PERISHED.

3 THE HOT AND COLD WATER CONNECTIONS
ARE LEAKING, EITHER AT THE WALL OR UNDER
THE SINK AT THE TAPS.

Job 18   LEAKING ROOF

Problem   WELL, EVERYONE'S GOT ONE OF THESE AND THEY'RE ANNOYING. I CALL THEM 'THE MOTHER-IN-LAW'.

Solution   THE LEAK COULD BE COMING FROM ANYWHERE SOMETIMES, AND IF IT'S NOT OBVIOUS, IT COULD BE HARD TO FIND. SO SEVEN TIMES OUT OF 10 YOU MAY NEED A PRO TO SOLVE IT 'CAUSE THE LAST THING YOU NEED IS TO FALL OFF THE ROOF. I'M THE FIRST PERSON TO SAY STAY OFF THE ROOF, BUT IF YOU'RE GONNA HAVE A GO, YOU MAY AS WELL KNOW WHAT YOU'RE DOING.

I WEAR SANDSHOES WITH A GOOD GRIP. NEVER GO UP THERE WHEN IT'S WET, AND ON A TILED ROOF WALK ON THE OVERLAPS TO AVOID BREAKING TILES.

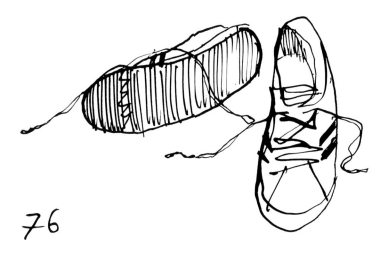

2 The most obvious cause of a roof leak is a broken tile or a hole in your tin roof. Hopefully you have a spare tile and can just replace it. Easy. But if you don't, you've got to match the tile up. There's a heap of patterns — some look identical but are shorter or longer, so make sure you match them up properly. As for a tin roof, if it's a small hole some ultraviolet-resistant silicone or similar will do the job. Larger than that a new sheet would be in order, and you may need a tradesman to install it for you. But at the end of the day, just stay off the roof.

Bernie's honeymoon 2

Bernie and the bride finally made it to the Lakes, out of the river system and into wide open water. The bride was smiling, Bernie was proud, his chest puffed up like a pancake.

The weather was looking a little nasty though. A bit of a chop on the Lakes kicked in. The wind started up from nowhere. But within 20 minutes it was like they were crossing the main street of Darwin in the middle of Cyclone Tracy in 1974. The tiny outboard was no match for the houseboat in the wind — they were going wherever the wind was taking them.

Bernie and the bride were like the Swiss Family Robinson, heading for the rocks on the bank. As they started to scrape the bank, Bernie ripped his shirt off and jumped in the water with a rope. Up the rocks he went, and tied the rope to a tree. With that, the wind spun round and blew the houseboat in the opposite direction. The tree wasn't big enough. The bride's on board, the rope won't hold in the wind and the rain is out of control.

There was a small restaurant a short distance away, so Bernie ran to get help. Through the rain he ran, at a 45-degree angle in the wind. No shirt, soaking wet and buggered, he burst into the restaurant panting and screaming, 'Help me! Help me! I've got my wife tied to a tree and the storm's going to rip it out!'

Luckily, there were two blokes in the joint who didn't think he was Jeffrey Dahmer and helped.

Afterwards, the locals said they couldn't understand the storm. They'd never seen anything like it. It was a freak of nature...They obviously didn't know Bernie was in town.

79

plumbing

Well, what a job — spending your day with other people's business. I did three years of a plumbing apprenticeship before going back to carpentry. I quite liked the trade and enjoyed my time messing about with pipes and poo. But don't panic, there's nothing to do with poo in this chapter. It's only the basics. Some of the solutions may not fit your problem — it's a bit hard without looking at it. The idea is to have a go and see if you can fix it and maybe save some money. If it doesn't work, you'll have to call the plumber. I'm sorry.

Job 1 FINDING THE METER

Problem CAN'T FIND THE WATER METER OR WHEN YOU FIND IT, IT WON'T TURN OFF PROPERLY.

Solution THE FIRST THING YOU SHOULD DO WHEN YOU MOVE INTO A NEW HOUSE OR UNIT IS FIND THE WATER METER AND CHECK IT TO MAKE SURE THE WASHER WORKS AND ACTUALLY SHUTS THE WATER DOWN. QUITE OFTEN YOU GO TO A WATER METER IN AN EMERGENCY AND IT NEEDS REPAIRS AND THE WATER CAN'T BE SHUT DOWN. IF THIS IS THE CASE, PUTTING A NEW WASHER IN THE METER IS UNFORTUNATELY A JOB FOR THE PLUMBER, BUT IT'S MONEY WELL SPENT. ONCE THE PIPE BURSTS IN THE KITCHEN, WATER GOING EVERYWHERE, YOU TURN THE WATER OFF AT THE MAIN AND NOTHING HAPPENS. CHECK IT AND GET IT FIXED.

1 THE WATER MAIN IS USUALLY ON THE LEFT-HAND SIDE OF THE FRONT YARD, OR IF YOU LIVE IN A UNIT IT CAN ACTUALLY BE IN THE UNIT. SOMETIMES IT'S IN THE KITCHEN

CABINET — JUST LOOK FOR A TAP UNDER A
CUPBOARD ON ITS OWN DOING NOTHING. TURN
IT OFF AND TEST THE WATER.

2 IF THERE'S A BURST
PIPE IN THE HOUSE AND
YOU GO TO THE METER,
BUT IT'S NOT SHUTTING
THE WATER DOWN
PROPERLY, WHAT DO YOU
DO? THERE'S USUALLY A
HOSE TAP RIGHT NEXT
TO THE METER. TURN IT ON FULL AS WELL AS
ANY OTHER TAP BETWEEN THE METER AND
THE BURST PIPE. THIS WILL REDUCE THE FLOW
IN THE HOUSE, NOT STOP IT, BUT IT MIGHT
SAVE A BIT OF CARPET TILL THE PLUMBER
SHOWS UP.

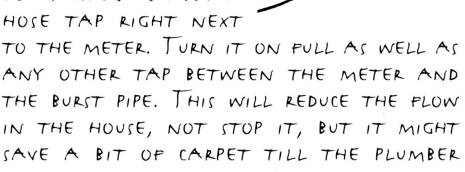

Arthur and the diet

It's always tough putting in a big day on the tools if you're not used to it, or if you're not fit. Here's a story about my old mate Arthur, the plumber, 19 stone and could eat enough for five blokes. Swollen legs, red face, heavy breathing when he watched paint dry.

We were working at Arthur's place one year when this van pulled up — Lite'N'Easy.

'What's the crack here, Arthur? Talk to me.'

He said to me, 'Well, I've made a decision. I'm gonna get fit, lose weight. I've seen all those "Before and After" shots and that's me.'

The boys all had a good laugh as Arthur nearly had a coronary carrying the boxes of food up the drive. This was about smoko time and Arthur said he couldn't eat until lunch. 'That's the new rules and I'm sticking to it.'

84

I thought, 'That poor bloke who owns the pie shop, he's gonna have to pull his kids out of school.'

Lunch time came around and Arthur set himself up in the kitchen to tuck into his first Lite'N'Easy lunch while me and the boys were outside eating.

Fifteen minutes went by. I wandered in and said, 'How ya going with the food, Arthur?'

He said, 'You're not going to believe this, Scotty, I'm full as a tick. I don't think I can finish this lunch. This diet is sensational.'

'Give us a look, Arthur...'

He'd eaten the entire week's lunches in the one sitting and was struggling through Sunday's.

'You knucklehead, Arthur.'

Job 2 NOISY PIPES

Problem WHEN YOU TURN THE TAP OFF — 'DONK!'
IT SOUNDS LIKE THE TAP'S ABOUT TO SNAP,
OFF. OR YOU GET THE 'TAP-TAP-TAP-TAP'
WHILE THE WATER'S RUNNING. THIS IS WATER
HAMMER, USUALLY DUE TO POOR INSTALLATION
OF PIPES.

Solution THE ONLY WAY YOU CAN FIX THIS, BEFORE
CALLING THE NEUROSURGEON, I MEAN THE
PLUMBER (I GET THEM MIXED UP 'CAUSE
THEY'RE PAID THE SAME), IS TO TRY TO
ISOLATE THE RATTLING PIPE AND TIGHTEN IT.
IF IT'S ATTACHED TO THE WALL OF YOUR FLOOR
FRAME WITHOUT ENOUGH FASTENINGS IT CAN
RATTLE AROUND WHEN YOU TURN YOUR TAPS
ON AND OFF.

1 FIND THE NOISE FIRST. GET UNDER THE HOUSE AND ASK YOUR HELPER TO TURN THE TAPS ON AND OFF.

2 IF THE PIPE IS LOOSE, SADDLE IT TO WHATEVER YOU CAN — BRICKWORK, BEARER, JOIST — AND ONCE YOU'VE DONE THAT, FLICK THE PIPE WITH YOUR FINGER AND LISTEN FOR ANY MOVEMENT.

3 KEEP WACKING THE SADDLES ON TILL IT'S TIGHT. THIS MAY NOT SOLVE THE ENTIRE PROBLEM AS THERE MAY BE LOOSE PIPES YOU CAN'T GET TO. IF IT'S STILL A PROBLEM, CALL THE DOCTOR (AH, PLUMBER) TO GET AN OPINION AND/OR QUOTE.

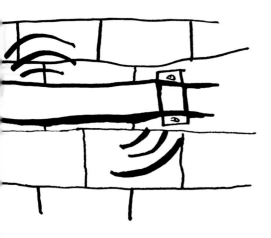

Job 3 BURST PIPE

Problem IF YOU'VE GOT SOME DAMP IN THE WALLS OR A WET SPOT IN THE GARDEN, YOU MAY HAVE A BURST PIPE.

Solution TO TEST FOR A BURST PIPE YOU CAN MARK THE METER AND CHECK IT THE NEXT DAY.

1 TURN ALL YOUR TAPS OFF NICE AND TIGHT BEFORE BED — AFTER ALL THE TEETH CLEANING, FACE WASHING AND ABLUTIONS — AND TURN OFF THE TOILETS AS THEY MAY HAVE A TINY LEAK YOU CAN'T SEE. YOU'LL STILL GET ONE FLUSH OUT OF EACH TOILET IN THE NIGHT.

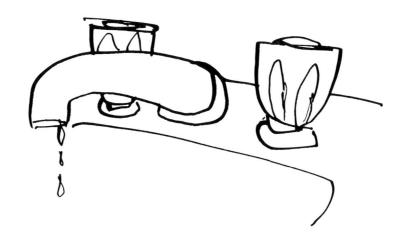

2 Whip out the front in your pyjamas with a texta and mark a line on the meter glass covering the numbers. Match what you've done on a piece of paper.

3 Go out again the next morning. Compare the position of the line on the meter with the one you copied onto paper the night before. If the line on the meter has moved since the night before, then obviously you have a water leak. When you call the plumber you can at least avoid the lengthy inspection costs and, if possible, you can dig up and expose the burst pipe to save even more.

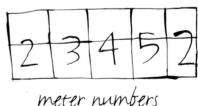

meter numbers

The water pump

I met a bloke in Western Australia who wanted to do up this old half cabin 30-foot jet boat and turn it into a charter dive boat. He had a bloke to do the mechanics and needed someone to do the timber work. I was George's man, and I did it on weekends and after work. He was a funny bloke, dry as, an old boatie from way back. George was in no hurry for the boat and we just plodded along.

I brought along a mate of mine, Andy Barthelson, and we worked on the boat every weekend until finally the launch date was set. She was called the Yorkshireman and looked fantastic.

We had a tractor and a big boat trailer, craned her on the trailer and took her the two blocks from my place to the ramp.

The trip up to the mooring from the ramp took about one hour. Four of us on board — myself and Andy, George and a young guy who worked for George. I had sorted out supplies — a big bag of kingies and two cases of cans. It was a proud day for Andy and me, the Yorkshireman finally hitting the water. We were puffed up like pancakes.

As she was launched, Andy stuck his penknife in one of the cans and sprayed Emu Bitter all over the bow. Seemed like a waste at the time, but I'm a big fan of tradition.

George fired the engines up and said, 'We're going five miles out, then we'll cut across to the mooring. We'll do a bit of fishing on the way.'

We were about four miles out, trawling a couple of lines. The young bloke had caught a nice queenie, I was on my third can, eating half a dozen prawns. The Yorkshireman was going great. It doesn't get any better than this.

Another boat was about 200 yards away. It was mates of ours on a fishing trip. Over the radio comes, 'Yorkshireman, Yorkshireman, you're sitting very low in the water. Over.

George replies, 'No worries, she sits low. Over.'

'Not that low, George — I reckon you're sinking. Over.'

It turns out that before our time the Yorkshireman used to have a dunny (or head, as it's called on boats). George ripped it out because you had to be one of the seven dwarfs to crawl in there to bury a pommie. It was easier to hang over the side. I had forgotten to turn off the stop valve of the waste pipe — the natural enemy of the inside of a boat. Water was coming in. At the end of the day we were sinking.

George lifted the hatch. All four of us said 'shit!' at the same time. The entire hull, up to three inches from the deck, was full of water and the level was rising fast. In a very gutsy (or stupid) move, the young bloke who worked for George jumped in the hatch, dived under, swam up the front in the pitch black, turned the valve off and saved the day.

George said, 'We're gonna have to get this water out or we'll sink in this swell.'

I said, 'George, there's no pumps in yet, we were putting them in tomorrow. How we gonna get the water out?'
He looked at Andy and me.

He said (dry as), 'There's no better water pump than two scared men with a bucket.'

Job 4 LEAKING TOILET

Problem YOU'RE GETTING WATER DRIPPING BEHIND THE SEAT WHEN YOU FLUSH.

Solution THIS IS USUALLY THE FLUSH CONE, THE LARGE RUBBER WASHER WHICH SEALS THE PIPE FROM THE CISTERN TO THE PAN. THIS EVENTUALLY PERISHES, SO IF YOURS LOOKS ALL CRACKED OR DRY, THAT'S YOUR PROBLEM.

1 CUT THE FLUSH CONE WITH A STANLEY KNIFE AND TAKE IT TO THE PLUMBING SUPPLY STORE TO MATCH IT TO A NEW ONE.

2 COVER THE INSIDE OF THE NEW CONE WITH VASOLINE AND SLIDE THE SMALL END OVER THE FLUSH PIPE. ROLL THE BIG END OF THE CONE BACKWARDS, TURNING IT INSIDE OUT. GET THE FLUSH PIPE BACK INTO POSITION INSIDE THE PAN INTAKE AND POP THE LARGE END OF THE CONE FORWARD. WRAP IT AROUND THE PAN INTAKE IN ONE HIT.

3 NOW JUST MASSAGE IT TO ADJUST IT AND THE JOB'S DONE.

flush cone

93

Job 5 RUNNING TOILET #1

Problem YOUR TOILET SOUNDS LIKE A FIVE-YEAR-OLD CONSTANTLY PEEING. IT'S DRIVING YOU MAD. WELL, FIX IT.

Solution THIS PROBLEM IS CAUSED BY A WORN CISTERN WASHER. IT'S A LITTLE COMPLICATED BUT WORTH HAVING A GO.

1 REMOVE THE LID OF THE CISTERN. SOMETIMES THERE'S SOMETHING STUCK UNDER

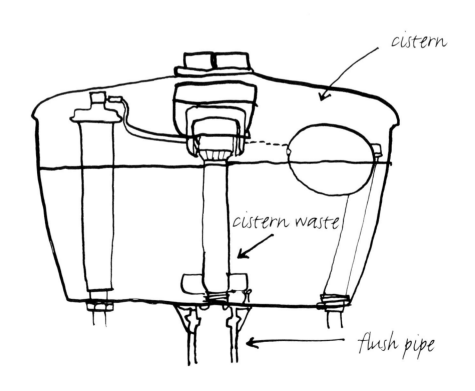

cistern

cistern waste

flush pipe

THE CISTERN WASHER, LETTING WATER OUT, LIKE AN OLD BLUE LOO CAPSULE OR SOMETHING. REMOVE IT, JOB'S DONE, BUT MORE LIKELY THE WASHER HAS PERISHED.

2 TURN THE TOILET OFF. THERE'S A TAP BEHIND THE TOILET WHICH CONTROLS THE FLOW OF WATER TO THE DUNNY.

3 FLUSH THE CISTERN. NOW YOU'LL HAVE A DRY UNIT. DOWN THE BOTTOM OF THE CISTERN, SEALING OFF THE ENTRANCE TO THE FLUSH PIPE, IS A WASHER. YOU CAN REACH IN AND PRISE THAT OFF.

4 TAKE IT TO THE PLUMBING SUPPLY STORE TO MATCH AND REPLACE IT. THERE COULD BE OTHER PROBLEMS CAUSING THIS, LIKE A PERISHED WASHER ON THE INTAKE, BUT THAT'S OVER THE PAGE ON THE NEXT JOB. THE NEW CISTERN WASHER IS CHEAP AS CHIPS SO IT CAN'T HURT TO REPLACE IT, 'CAUSE IF ONE'S GONE THE OTHER WILL GO SOON.

plumbing

Job 6 RUNNING TOILET #2

Problem THE TOILET'S STILL RUNNING, AND NOW YOU NEED TO GO. FIX IT.

Solution BESIDES THE CISTERN WASHER, YOUR RUNNY DUNNY COULD ALSO BE DUE TO THE WATER INTAKE WASHER.

1 TAKE THE CISTERN LID OFF, PUSH DOWN ON THE FLOAT AND LISTEN FOR THE WATER COMING IN. THAT'S THE WATER INTAKE.

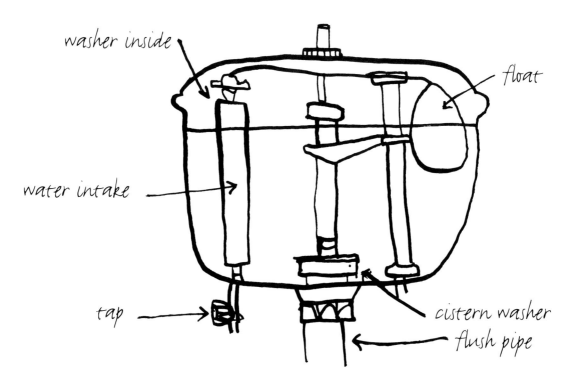

washer inside

float

water intake

tap

cistern washer
flush pipe

96

2 Turn the water to the toilet off and flush the toilet. This will give you a dry unit.

3 Remove the float arm from the water intake — this is normally a plastic split pin or screw.

4 Unscrew the top of the water intake. There will be a washer in the top. As usual, with all plumbing fittings there are 10,000 different types, so take it down to the supplier and match it up.

5 Replace the washer, put it all back together and you're away.

Bernie and the fart box

I did a show a few years back which involved a couple of great blokes who had cystic fibrosis. They dressed up as clowns and entertained the younger kiddies with the same affliction. Peeboow and Dagwood — two of the nicest and funniest guys (who were twins), with the best attitude to life under tough conditions you'd ever want to meet.

They had this fart box with a little remote control unit. When you hit the button a very realistic fart would pop out. It had six different farts and was only about the size of a mobile phone. The kids loved it, and so did I.

And through their generosity Peeboow and Dagwood gave me one. My new, prized possession.

Straight up the pub with it. Hid the unit amongst the straws on the bar next to the till. When one of

98

the boys went up for
a shout and the
good sort behind
the bar was at the till
about to give him some
change, I'd hit the
button in my pocket. Out ripped a
beauty. Everyone was blaming everyone else. Zolly
came back from the bar, saying, 'Boys, you should
have heard the fart that good sort just did.'

When it came out that it was the fart box, the
Table of Knowledge loved it. Bernie thought it was
hilarious and spotted a bloke right over in the other
corner, reading the paper with his back to us.
Bernie grabbed the box and danced over on tippy
toes, snuck up behind him and slotted the box right
under his chair.

He ran back, all excited and bouncing up and
down, begging for the button.

I said, 'Bernie, are you out of ya mind? We don't
even know this bloke. He might take offence.

Go and get it, you knucklehead.'

Bernie's excitement dropped like a stone. Head down, he said, 'Yeah, you're right. Sorry...'

The Table knew what I was up to. As Bernie slowly bent down under this bloke's chair and went down on his hands and knees, I hit the button. 'Riiiippp.' A little pause, then another.

The guy dropped his paper and turned in shock to see Bernie crouching behind his chair with a stupid grin on his face.

Bernie came back to us, shaking his head and saying, 'I knew you were going to do that.'

Oh, McGoo.

Job 7 BLOCKED TOILET

Problem OH-OH...FAMILY OF FIVE, 8 AM, BIG CHINESE FEED LAST NIGHT, DUNNY'S BLOCKED. PLUMBER SAYS, 'I'LL BE ABOUT AN HOUR.' 'WERE YOU BORN ON MARS? WE HAVEN'T GOT AN HOUR!' MUST THINK OF SOMETHING.

Solution THIS DOESN'T ALWAYS WORK, BUT IT HAS FOR ME. AND IT'LL BUY YOU SOME TIME UNTIL THE PLUMBER ARRIVES TO EEL THINGS AWAY.

GRAB YOURSELF A WHITE HAIR MOP. IF YOU HAVEN'T GOT ONE, YOU'RE RIGHT IN THE SHIT. STICK IT IN THE PAN, AND PUMP IT BACK AND FORTH AS HARD AS YOU CAN. IT WILL MOVE THINGS DOWN THE LINE A BIT, BUT IF YOUR BLOCKAGE IS MAJOR IT MAY DO NOTHING.

AND BE PREPARED FOR A FEW SPLASHES. TOUGHEN UP, YOU'VE GOT A FAMILY FULL OF PEKING DUCK THAT'S BUSTING TO SEE THE LIGHT OF DAY.

101

Job 8 REPLACING A TOILET SEAT

Problem NOTHING WORSE THAN TRYING TO CONCENTRATE ON THE FOOTY RESULTS, AND YOUR BUM KEEPS SLIPPING SIDEWAYS.

Solution IT DOESN'T GET ANY EASIER THAN THIS. THE BEST PLACE TO PURCHASE THE NEW SEAT IS AT THE PLUMBING SUPPLY STORE 'CAUSE THEY HAVE THE BEST RANGE.

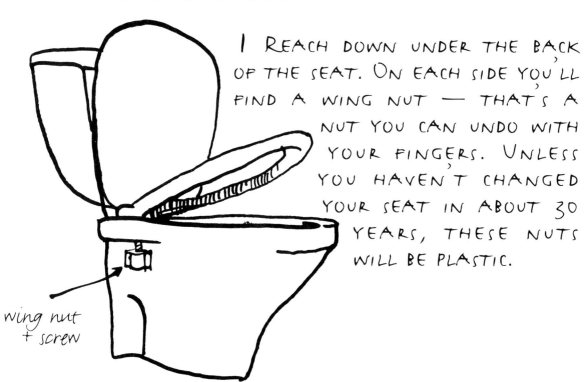

1 REACH DOWN UNDER THE BACK OF THE SEAT. ON EACH SIDE YOU'LL FIND A WING NUT — THAT'S A NUT YOU CAN UNDO WITH YOUR FINGERS. UNLESS YOU HAVEN'T CHANGED YOUR SEAT IN ABOUT 30 YEARS, THESE NUTS WILL BE PLASTIC.

wing nut + screw

2 THE NEW SEAT COMES WITH NEW SCREWS AND WING NUTS.

Dave and the dunny seat ring

A GOOD MATE OF MINE GOT HIMSELF A POOL. WE WENT OVER THERE FOR THE FIRST DAY OF SWIMMING. MY MATE DISAPPEARED FOR ABOUT 10 MINUTES IN THE BUDGIE SMUGGLERS (SPEEDOS). WHEN HE CAME BACK HE HAD THE BIG RED DUNNY SEAT RING AROUND THE TOP OF HIS LEGS. WE JUST LEFT HIM TO RUN AROUND THE YARD WHILE WE HAD A GOOD LAUGH. I WON'T MENTION ANY NAMES, DAVE.

Bernie's overseas holiday

Bernie and the bride aren't the best travellers. Something always goes wrong. Lost bags, lost wife, the houseboat's going the wrong way — that sort of thing. Bernie and the missus aren't big on flying either — too cramped, restless, deep vein thrombosis. Bernie brings all these things up on the Table of Knowledge, and gets the standard response: 'Oh shut up, Bern.'

He's got the nine-hour flight coming up, taking the bride on the trip of a lifetime. It's all going to be great, except for the flight — but this time it's going to be different. 'How's that, Bernie?' Old Bernie Boy's got himself a mate who's a doctor. He got these pills for Bernie and the bride which are going to make them sleep for five hours. Half the flight sleeping, the other half a few beers, the movie...maybe sleep the whole way...

Bernie and the bride board the plane, all excited, pills at the ready. The bride has a bottle of water. As soon as they sit down, the seat belts go on and the pills go down. Bernie convinces the bride they should take two so they can sleep twice as long. Within 15 minutes, before the plane even moves, Bernie and the bride are counting sheep.

The plane takes off with Bernie and the bride still asleep. But while they're asleep the pilot decides to circle around and land back at the airport to have something checked out.

Thinking the delay won't be long, the stewards keep the passengers on board the plane. Finally, the plane taxies out to the runway.

You know what's coming — Bernie and the bride wake up. Sore backs, numb arses. 'Where are we? What's happening?' Asleep for four and a half hours and they haven't even left the airport.

Nine hours later, Bernie and the bride landed again. They were that buggered, they slept through the first day of a seven-day holiday. You've gotta laugh at knucklehead Bernie. It always happens to him.

Job 9 HOSES AND FITTINGS

Problem YOUR HOSE WON'T LAST FOREVER (THAT'S WHAT THE MISSUS TOLD ME). SO IF YOU'RE HAVING TROUBLE WITH KINKS AND A HARD BRITTLE HOSE, GET RID OF IT.

Solution AS FAR AS FITTINGS GO, ALWAYS BUY QUALITY. THAT GOES FOR EVERYTHING WE'VE TALKED ABOUT. RECENTLY I BOUGHT CHEAP PLASTIC FITTINGS AND WITHIN THE MONTH I HAD TO REPLACE THE TAP CONNECTOR TWICE.

THERE ARE BRASS HOSE FITTINGS — A BIT MORE OUT OF THE POCKET, BUT WORTH IT IN THE END. I REMEMBER AN OLD SAYING OF MY DAD'S: 'YOU'RE AN IDIOT, SCOTT. BUY BRASS.'

Tip
MOST GARDEN TAPS ARE 3/4 INCH, BUT YOU CAN GET 1/2 INCH — THAT'S WHY THE HOSE TAP FITTING COMES WITH A 1/2 INCH ADAPTOR. IT'S AN INSERT OR BUSH INSIDE THE THREAD. SO WHEN YOU BUY YOUR FITTING AND YOU'VE GOT A 3/4 INCH TAP, JUST UNSCREW THE 1/2 INCH BUSH AND YOUR FITTING BECOMES 3/4 INCH.

Job 10 SHOWER CURTAIN ROD

Problem YOU ARRIVE AT THE NEW JOINT AND THERE'S NO SHOWER ROD.

Solution HERE'S A CHEAP WAY TO SORT OUT THE ROD AND BE ABLE TO TAKE IT WITH YOU. THERE ARE ALWAYS TWO WALLS EITHER SIDE OF YOUR BATH/SHOWER. YOU CAN BUY AN ADJUSTABLE SHOWER ROD THAT'S STRAIGHT. BUT YOU DON'T NEED TO BUY ONE WHEN YOU CAN TAKE THE BULL BY THE HORNS AND MAKE ONE.

screw

stopper

1 MEASURE THE WIDTH BETWEEN WALLS, THEN BUY AND CUT A PIECE OF 20 MM (3/4 IN) DOWEL 20 MM (3/4 IN) SHORTER.

2 PUT A SCREW INTO ONE END, LEAVING ABOUT 17 MM (2/3 IN) PROUD.

3 FIND TWO BITS OF RUBBER ABOUT 5 MM (1/4 IN) THICK. GLUE ONE PIECE TO ONE END OF THE DOWEL. PUT THE OTHER PIECE BETWEEN THE WALL AND THE SCREW. JUST ADJUST THE SCREW UNTIL IT'S A NICE TIGHT FIT. ONE SHOWER CURTAIN ROD.

Job 11 DRIPPING SHOWER ROSE

Problem YOU TURN THE SHOWER ON. YOU'VE GOT THE COLD BEER IN THE SHOWER SITTING ON THE SHELF YOU BUILT FOR IT — EVERYTHING'S PERFECT. BUT YOU'VE GOT THAT ANNOYING SPRAY OF WATER GOING SIDEWAYS OUT OF THE TOP OF THE SHOWER ROSE. ALL OVER THE SECOND BEER SITTING ON THE VANITY. I ALWAYS HAVE A TWO-BEER SHOWER IN SUMMER — THERE'S NOTHING FINER. ONE BEER FOR WAIST UP AND ONE FOR WAIST DOWN, WHICH INCLUDES STANDING UNDER THE SHOWER FOR FIVE MINUTES DOING NOTHING.

Solution THE SIDEWAYS SPRAY IS EASILY FIXED BY THREAD TAPE.

I UNSCREW THE ROSE. MOST MODERN ROSES HAVE A WASHER — JUST REPLACE IT. SOME ARE HINGED AND THEY LEAK RIGHT AT THE ELBOW. THESE ALSO HAVE A WASHER — REPLACE IT.

2 If it's leaking where there is just threaded pipe (like a bolt), thread tape is needed. Thread tape is cheap — it's like sticky tape with no sticky. Just undo the fitting, expose the thread and wrap thread tape around it, probably about 10 times. Put the fitting back on the thread tape. Now the joins are sealed. No more leaks. Time for a second beer.

Paddle-pops

One of the first rules of a tradesman is — when you're in someone's house, don't touch anything. You're not supposed to.

An old plumber mate of mine broke that rule and got in real strife.

He was sent out to a job by the boss and was told the key was under the mat. This sort of thing happened all the time with regular clients.

Ol' Mate got to the joint and started setting up. He was starving on account of all the schooners he'd had the night before. The can of black aspro (Coca-Cola) wasn't working; he needed some food. Since no one was home, he went straight for the pantry. One biscuit from each tin...no one will notice one slice of cheese, almost got a full meal here. The theory was one item from every food group...no one will notice.

He'd opened up the freezer to see four magnificent icy-cold chocolate paddle-pops. Only four, it's a risk...she'll never notice...I shouldn't...only four...if only there were eight...no dramas...Bugger it, she'll never notice it.

He finished his gourmet bicky and bread and cheese meal, and then hoed into dessert. Just as he was concealing the paddle-pop stick in the tool box, the door opened, and Mum and the four kids came running in, with Mum yelling at them, 'I've got a surprise for you kids in the freezer!'

Ol' Mate stood by in horror as the kids danced around the freezer and Mum searched for the fourth paddle- pop. Then she pulled her head out of the freezer and looked straight at him.

Busted.

The knucklehead lost his job.

Job 12 SEALING GAPS IN THE BATHROOM

Problem THERE'S A GAP BETWEEN THE BATH AND THE BOTTOM TILE, OR IN THE CORNER OF THE SHOWER. IF YOU DON'T FIX IT, THE WATER'S GOING TO LEAK INTO THE WALL.

Solution WHEREVER YOU GET TWO SURFACES MEETING, LIKE A CORNER IN A SHOWER OR THE TOP OF THE BATH, USE A FLEXIBLE GAP FILLER

gap

gap

INSTEAD OF REPLACING THESE GAPS WITH TILE GROUT. BUT MAKE SURE IT'S SUITABLE FOR TILES AND WET AREAS. YOUR LOCAL TILE SHOP WILL BE ABLE TO HELP.

1 GET YOURSELF A CAULKING GUN AND WACK THE TUBE OF FILLER IN.

2 APPLY A THIN LINE OF FILLER ALONG THE GAP AND SMOOTH IT OFF WITH A WET FINGER.

REMEMBER, WHEN DOING SOMETHING SPECIFIC TO A PARTICULAR TRADE, THE GUYS AT THE SHOP WILL ALWAYS SUPPLY MORE PROFESSIONAL INFORMATION ON PRODUCTS TO THAT TRADE.

Corn on the head

Years ago I worked as the house carpenter in a resort in northern Western Australia. But that meant you put your hand to everything that was broken.

We had a bit of a drama with the sewerage system at the resort, and the ladies' toilets by the pool were backing up.

Kevin, a bloke I used to work with and still remain terrific friends with to this day, was called on by the boss to have a look. He dragged me along 'cause I'd done a bit of plumbing.

Kev was about 50 years old and the nicest bloke you'd ever want to meet. I was about 25 so Kev taught me a lot, but he treated me as an equal. I've always thought that's the best way to teach young blokes. They tend to want to learn more so they don't let you down.

If that's not the best wrap you ever get, Kev, then I'm drinking a Pimm's and lemonade. Kev is 65 now and a cranky old bastard. I can't be nice to him — he'll think I'm going soft.

Anyway Kev and I wander down the hill and find an IO in the pipe. That's an inspection opening with a screwed-on cap. We needed to open that cap and check the line to see where the blockage was.

We both looked at the cap and sensed it was under pressure. There was about 100 metres of buildup and it was busting at the seams to get out.

Kev said, 'Right. Take the cap off, mate.'

I said, 'Hang on a minute. This is your job. I'm just helping, remember.' Kev had a great knack of making you feel guilty. He'd say, 'Oh! I'm sorry, mate. I didn't mean to assume...' In the end you'd say, 'Get out of the way. I'll do it.'

Slowly, I bent down towards the inspection cap. Unscrewing the cap an inch at a time, it was like defusing a bomb. Kev had his hands on his knees with a nervous look on his face. I was waiting for him to scream, 'Cut the blue wire, the blue!!'

I was on the last thread of the screwed cap. I gave it an extra turn and 'Ka-boom!' The lid shot up about 10 feet and out roared water, paper, shit and whatever else. It was like the Kiama blowhole.

I managed to jump out of the way and copped a few splashes. No dramas. Kev had been crouching and staring at the 10 for so long I think his knees locked up a bit and he didn't fare so well. Basically he

copped the lot. We both laughed — me much harder than him — then I walked over to Kev and looked him in the eye.

He said, 'What?' Kev was balding and right in the middle of his head was a corn kernel. I reached up with a screwdriver, gently scooped it up and brought it down right in front of his eye — 'That's what!'

Kev bolted — dry retching up the hill — while I almost added to the mess from laughing so much.

Kev and I went back to our respective houses, showered, then ran a bath of Dettol to lie in.

Job 13 BROKEN BATHROOM TILE

Problem YOU SLIPPED OVER IN THE SHOWER AND YOUR STUBBY BUSTED A TILE.

Solution BE AWARE THAT THIS COULD END UP HAVING A SNOWBALL EFFECT — AS YOU CHIP AWAY AT THE CRACKED TILE, YOU COULD END UP CHIPPING OR CRACKING THE TILES EITHER SIDE OF IT, AND SO ON AND SO ON. BE VERY CAREFUL.

1 AN IMPORTANT SAFETY TIP — ALWAYS WEAR SAFETY GOGGLES. TILES SPLINTER OFF LIKE GLASS AND LODGE STRAIGHT IN THE OLD EYEBALL. AND WEAR LONG SLEEVES AND LONG PANTS — A LARGER PIECE OF TILE FALLING OFF THE WALL CAN CUT YOU OPEN LIKE A RAZOR. A MATE OF MINE GOT 12 STITCHES IN THE THIGH FROM EXACTLY THAT.

2 USING AN OLD SCREWDRIVER, CLEAN OUT THE GROUT FROM AROUND THE TILE. SCRAPE AWAY UNTIL IT'S FAIRLY CLEAN. DOESN'T HAVE TO BE PERFECT.

3 Using the screwdriver and a hammer, gently tap away at the tile. Start from the crack, preferably in the middle of the tile. Never start at the grout line and work in. Always start in the middle and work out.

4 You can buy a 1 L (2 pt) container of pre-mixed tile adhesive or you can even use silicone. If you do, keep it away from the edges so it doesn't squash into the grout lines. Next, tile in.

5 Mix up your grout until it feels like toothpaste and grout away. Wipe off the excess...job's done.

plumbing

Job 14 WET PATCH ON THE BEDROOM WALL

Problem IN OLD PLACES WITH UNRENOVATED BATHROOMS THIS IS THE MOST COMMON PROBLEM I SEE.

Solution THE WET PATCH JUST ABOUT ALWAYS LINES UP WITH THE SHOWER OR BATH — THE WATER PENETRATES THE SHOWER WALL AND COMES OUT BY PEELING THE PAINT ON THE BEDROOM WALL NEXT DOOR.

THE MOST COMMON CAUSE OF THIS PROBLEM IS MISSING GROUT IN THE TILES. SO CHECK THIS AND RE-GROUT ALL THE BATHROOM WALLS. AND REMEMBER TO USE FLEXIBLE GROUT IN THE CORNERS.

ANOTHER COMMON REASON IS THAT THE TAPWARE IN THE SHOWER OR BATH IS NOT SEALED BEHIND THE FLANGES.

1 PULL YOUR TAP HANDLE OFF. THE FLANGE WILL EITHER UNSCREW OR COME OFF WITH A PLASTIC CAP THAT KEEPS THE SPRING PUSHING

120

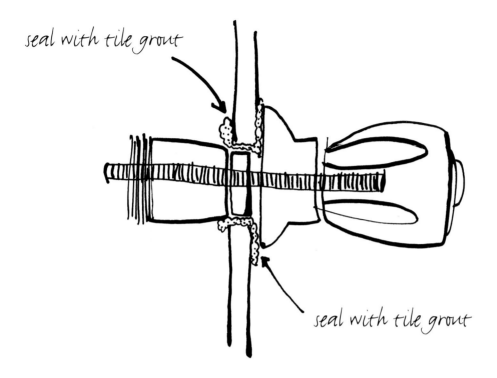

seal with tile grout

seal with tile grout

ON THE FLANGE. PULL THE PLASTIC CAP OFF,
AND THE SPRING AND FLANGE WILL COME
WITH IT!

2 NOW YOU HAVE AN EXPOSED SPINDLE. IF
THERE ARE GAPS, AND YOU CAN SEE RENDER
OR BRICKWORK, SEAL THAT AREA UP WITH
TILE GROUT.

IF THESE SUGGESTIONS DON'T WORK, YOU MAY
HAVE A BURST PIPE AND A PLUMBER IS THE GO.

Job 15 UPSTAIRS BATHROOM LEAKING

Problem THERE'S A DRIP CONSTANTLY HITTING THE DINNER TABLE, AND THE UPSTAIRS BATHROOM IS RIGHT OVERHEAD.

Solution THIS IS A REAL PROBLEM, AND A NUMBER OF THINGS COULD BE CAUSING IT.

MOST OF THE TIME IT'S INADEQUATE WATERPROOFING BEFORE THE TILING WENT DOWN — IN VERY OLD SECOND-STOREY BATHROOMS, WATERPROOFING TECHNIQUES WEREN'T AS GOOD AS THEY ARE NOW.

EVEN THOUGH THE PRODUCTS HAVE IMPROVED, IT DOESN'T MEAN THAT YOU CAN GET AWAY WITH POOR APPLICATION.

THERE SHOULD BE A CEILING SPACE BELOW THE BATHROOM SO YOU CAN ACCESS THE PIPE WORK. A MANHOLE SHOULD BE CUT SO A VISUAL INSPECTION CAN BE DONE.

JOB 15

THIS IS A PROFESSIONAL JOB, AND YOU SHOULD
BRING IN A PLUMBER AND/OR A BUILDER AS
SOON AS POSSIBLE, BEFORE ANY FURTHER
DAMAGE OCCURS.

IT'S ONE OF THE NASTY JOBS AROUND, BECAUSE
IF THE PROBLEM IS BAD IT COULD MEAN
LIFTING ALL THE TILES AND REDOING THE
WATERPROOFING. HOPEFULLY, THE PLUMBER
WILL FIND A SIMPLE (AND CHEAP) SOLUTION.

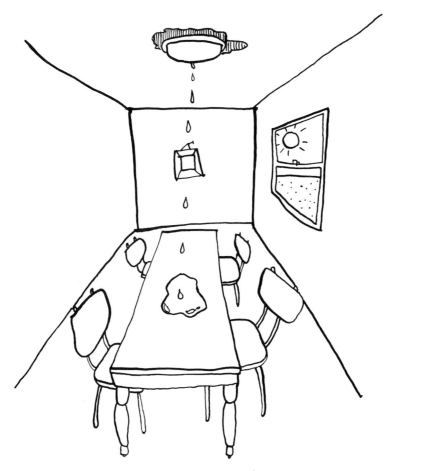

The bank robbery

I've always fancied myself as the hero in the situation where the lady has her bag snatched, I jump across and coathanger the bloke, save the day and end up in the human interest section of the Telegraph, saying, 'I don't consider myself a hero. I just did what any other bloke would do.'

When it all comes down to it, I'd probably drop my bundle and let the guy run right past, saying to myself for the next month, 'If only I'd coathangered that knucklehead...'

This story is not the full monty but it's as close as you'll get.

I was driving my ute through Bondi Junction with my girlfriend, nice day, everything calm, when these two wankers sprinted out in front of me, made me lock up the ute. All my tools fell forward, the girlfriend got a little seat belt bruise on one of her not so little lungs. I was filthy. I could've killed those two blokes and I gave them a gobful.

There was something different about these two blokes. They were carrying a small bag, and they had sheer panic on their faces. As they got across the road they jumped into a waiting Commodore V8. When the driver took off he left one bloke behind, hanging on to the door. He was out there, swinging in the breeze, as they drove off. The others dragged him in on the move. I thought, 'That's gotta be Brocky doing his shopping.'

But I looked left. There's the Commonwealth Bank and the boys had been sprinting out of the side doors. It all gelled.

'They've just robbed the bank!' I screamed at the girlfriend. They were all looking at us as I was giving them the gobful and Ann (the girlfriend) screamed back at me, 'Let them go! Let them go!'

Not me. I could see that human interest story, with the picture of the bank manager giving me one of those giant cheques for saving the day.

Back to second gear and I floored it. We were right up there, clacker dodging through traffic. In those days I had the in-car phone with the hands-free. I belted out 000 and got onto this policewoman.

'How can I help you?'

Now I was going flat strap, red-lining the ute, changing gears, so it was pretty noisy. I would've sounded like Brocky when he's got the in-car camera at Bathurst. Anyway, I came back to the policewoman with: 'I'm in hot pursuit, west-bound on Moore Park Road. I have a visual on four male Caucasians who just robbed a bank, in a white Calais Commodore, licence plate...' (here's where it gets good), '...Charlie, Alfa, Sierra, oner, fourer, twoa.' I learnt all that from my Adam 12 watching days.

She came back with, 'Pull over, immediately.'

126

'Negative.' Ann looked at me at this point and realised I'd lost the plot.

'Negative, we're now turning left into Lang Road. I may lose them on the speed bumps.'

'Pull over, driver.'

'I've lost them. They're heading south doing about 120 km/h. I've pulled over...'

The policewoman said, 'Can I have your name and address, please?'

Suddenly I snapped out of Adam 12 mode and said, 'I don't think so,' and hung up. The chase was over. We sat there for a few seconds, then Ann punched me in the arm, called me a 'f*******
wanker' and we went home. What a great arvo.

plumbing

Job 16 BLOCKED SINK

Problem   IF YOU COULD SEE INSIDE YOUR SINK TRAP, WHICH IS THE CURVY PIPE UNDER YOUR SINK, YOU'D NEVER USE IT AGAIN. IT IS A DISGRACE, IT'S HORRIBLE — THE WORST SMELL, GREASE, SLIME.

Solution   THAT'S WHY YOU HAVE A TRAP, 'CAUSE THE CURVED BIT HOLDS WATER AND STOPS THE SMELL. IF YOU HAVE A BLOCKED SINK, IT'S USUALLY A BUILDUP OF GREASE AND OTHER NASTY GEAR IN THE TRAP.

GIVE THE CHEMICALS (PROPRIETARY DRAIN CLEANERS) A GO — BUT THEY DON'T ALWAYS DO THE FULL JOB.

1 TAKE THE TRAP OFF.

2 DISCONNECT THE TOP AND BOTTOM, AND CLEAN OUT THE TRAP. IF IT'S CLEAN, THE BLOCKAGE WILL BE FURTHER DOWN THE LINE, SO THE PLUMBER WILL BE THE GO.

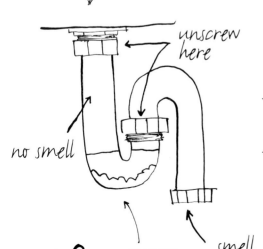

sink

unscrew here

no smell

grease   smell

128

Job 17 THE TPR VALVE

Problem

THE TPR VALVE CAN DRIP FOR A SHORT WHILE EVERY NOW AND THEN — THAT'S ITS JOB — BUT IF IT'S LEAKING CONSTANTLY IT NEEDS REPLACING. THIS IS A PLUMBER'S JOB.

Solution

ALL TANK-STYLE HOT WATER SYSTEMS HAVE A TEMPERATURE PRESSURE RELIEF (TPR) VALVE. THIS IS THE VALVE ON THE SIDE OF THE HOT WATER TANK. IT HAS ABOUT 1 M (3 FT) OF COPPER PIPE ATTACHED TO IT. THE PIPE BENDS OUT OF THE BOTTOM OF THE TANK AND FEEDS ONTO THE GROUND. IF THE TANK IS INSIDE, THIS PIPE WILL FEED OUTSIDE THROUGH A SMALL HOLE IN THE EXTERNAL WALLS.

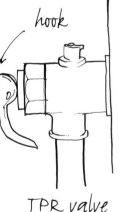

hook

TPR valve

BASICALLY, THIS VALVE STOPS THE TANK FROM BUILDING UP PRESSURE AND BLOWING UP — AS THE NAME SUGGESTS, IT RELIEVES PRESSURE.

ABOUT EVERY THREE MONTHS, PULL THE HOOK ON THE VALVE FOR TWO SECONDS OR SO. HOT WATER WILL COME OUT OF THE PIPE. SO WATCH YOUR FEET, THIS JUST TESTS IT TO MAKE SURE THE VALVE'S NOT SEIZED UP.

Job 18 INSTALLING A DISHWASHER

Problem THE WIFE WANTS THE NEW DISHWASHER INSTALLED NOW!

Solution I'M ASSUMING ALL THE NECESSARY DISHWASHER FITTINGS ARE THERE. IF NOT, A PLUMBER IS REQUIRED. BUT IF THEY ARE THERE, YOU'RE AWAY.

1 THE WATER INTAKE IS THE SAME AS THE ONE ON THE WASHING MACHINE. JUST SCREW THAT ONTO THE TAP FITTING UNDER THE SINK.

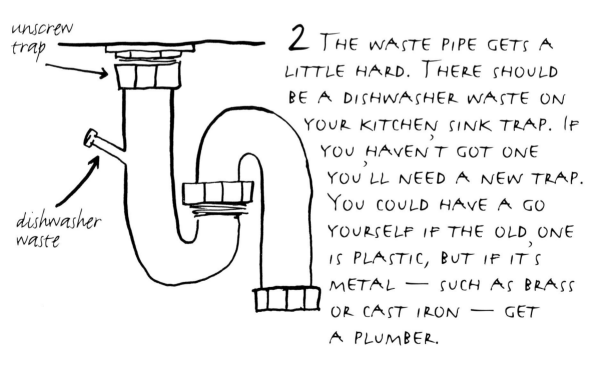

unscrew trap

dishwasher waste

2 THE WASTE PIPE GETS A LITTLE HARD. THERE SHOULD BE A DISHWASHER WASTE ON YOUR KITCHEN SINK TRAP. IF YOU HAVEN'T GOT ONE YOU'LL NEED A NEW TRAP. YOU COULD HAVE A GO YOURSELF IF THE OLD ONE IS PLASTIC, BUT IF IT'S METAL — SUCH AS BRASS OR CAST IRON — GET A PLUMBER.

3 The most important thing to check is that the dishwasher waste on the trap has been drilled out. When the traps are new they are sealed. A 10 mm ($\frac{1}{2}$ in) hole is enough.

hose clamp

4 Pop the dishwasher waste on with a hose clamp, and then tighten it up with a screwdriver.

5 Then comes the most important thing. Get someone else to stack the dishwasher.

Job 19 DRIPPING EAVES

Problem WHAT IS THAT WATER DRIPPING OUT OF THE PIPE UNDER MY EAVES?

Solution THIS ONE IS A REGULAR OCCURRENCE AND I SEE IT ALL THE TIME, USUALLY IN OLD HOUSES. IT MEANS YOU HAVE A GRAVITY-FED HOT WATER UNIT — A LARGE TANK IN THE CEILING WITH THE HOT WATER BEING FED DOWN BY GRAVITY.

I GREW UP WITH ONE OF THESE AND THOUGHT EVERY SHOWER HAD A FEEBLE PRESSURE, UNTIL I WAS ABOUT 17 AND STAYED AT A MATE'S PLACE WHERE THE OUTSIDE TANK HAD A MAINS PRESSURE HOOKED TO IT. I WAS LOOKING FOR THE SEAT BELT, COULDN'T BELIEVE THE PRESSURE. HIS OLD MAN HAD TO GO CROOK ON ME TO GET ME OUT.

ON THE SIDE OF THESE TANKS IS A UNIT VIRTUALLY IDENTICAL TO A TOILET CISTERN. IT REGULATES THE FLOW OF WATER IN THE TANK. THE WATER DRIPPING OUT OF THE EAVES IS THE OVERFLOW PIPE — IT'S LIKE A RUNNING

TOILET AND IT MEANS ONE OF THE WASHERS IN THE UNIT HAS PERISHED AND NEEDS TO BE REPLACED. HAVE A GO AT FIXING IT BY CHECKING OUT THE TOILET CISTERN PROBLEM (JOB 5) AND ADAPTING THAT METHOD. IF YOU CAN'T FIGURE IT OUT, GET THE PLUMBER IN.

THE CRUCIAL THING ABOUT THIS IS THAT IT'S HOT WATER DRIPPING OUT OF THERE AND IT'S COSTING YOU DOUGH.

I'VE SEEN ONE OF THESE PIPES FLOWING LIKE A TAP WITH STEAM COMING OFF IT AND THE BLOKE SAYING, 'IT'S BEEN LIKE THAT FOR 12 MONTHS.' KNUCKLEHEAD.

Job 20 RUSTY HOLES IN THE GUTTER

Problem YOU FORGET ALL ABOUT THIS PROBLEM, UNTIL IT RAINS.

Solution THIS ONE CAN GET TOUGH, SO READ CAREFULLY.

1 CUT OUT THE RUSTY SECTION OF THE GUTTER WITH TIN SNIPS AND A HACKSAW. BEND UP THE TIPS OF THE GUTTER BRACKETS IN THE RUSTY AREA AND POP OUT THE RUSTY SECTION.

2 LOOK OUT FOR ANY BENT OVER NAILS IN THE BACK OF THE GUTTER — PLUMBERS USED TO DO THAT TO HOLD THE GUTTER.

3 NOW FOR THE TOUGH PART. CUT THE NEW PIECE OF GUTTER ABOUT 300 MM (12 IN) LONGER THAN THE OPENING, 'CAUSE YOU HAVE TO ALLOW FOR OVERLAP.

4 FIND OUT WHICH WAY YOUR FALL IS GOING. THE FALL IS THE SLOPE OF THE GUTTER, SO THE WATER RUNS OUT OF THE GUTTER INSTEAD

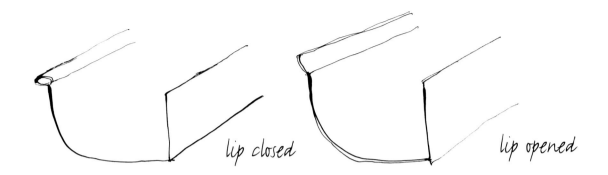

lip closed   *lip opened*

OF SITTING THERE. THE NEW PIECE OF GUTTER
GOES UNDERNEATH THE HIGH SIDE AND SITS ON
THE INSIDE OF THE LOW SIDE. THE ROLL AT
THE TOP OF THE GUTTER MUST BE OPENED UP
WITH MULTIGRIPS OR PLIERS.

5 OPEN UP THE ROLL ON THE OLD GUTTER ON
THE HIGH SIDE AND THE ROLL ON THE NEW
PIECE ON THE LOW SIDE. JUST OPEN ENOUGH TO
COVER THE OVERLAP. SQUIRT A LINE OF GUTTER
SILICONE ON THE INSIDE OF THE GUTTER IN
THE MIDDLE OF BOTH OVERLAPS, FIT THE NEW
GUTTER IN POSITION AND BEND BACK THE
ROLLS. SILICONE UP THE JOINS ON THE INSIDE
ONLY, AND BEND BACK YOUR GUTTER BRACKETS.
NO MORE LEAKS.

Plastering

Plastering is one of those trades where there's 'a bit of an art to it'. You need practice. So expect the first couple of jobs to be a bit ordinary until you get the hang of it. Start off with very small jobs and work up to the bigger ones. But don't be fooled into taking on the big jobs straightaway, 'cause a dud plastering job stands out like dog balls on a canary.

plastering

Job 1 PATCHING A HOLE IN GYPROCK

Problem You're playing footy in the lounge room, when all of a sudden, you put your elbow through the wall trying to catch the ball.

Solution Gyprock is covered in paper on both sides so a hole is rarely neat.

1 Using a Stanley knife, cut out the gyprock that's pushed in and hanging on. Basically, neaten and clean up the hole.

2 Measure the diameter of the hole, then cut a strip of new gyprock so that the width is 10 mm (1/2 in) shorter than the diameter, and the length of the strip is 50 mm (2 in) longer than the diameter. So if the hole has a diameter of 80 mm (3 in), the strip is 130 x 70 mm (5 x 3 in) — too easy.

3 Gently insert a screw in the centre of the strip, but only to the depth of the

GYPROCK, LEAVING ENOUGH SCREW STICKING OUT TO GRAB ON TO.

4 YOU'LL NEED CORNICE CEMENT. YOU CAN BUY 2 KG (4.4 LB) BAGS FAIRLY CHEAP. MIX ABOUT TWO HANDFULS INTO A NICE PASTE. ONCE YOU'VE MIXED IT UP, YOU HAVE TO WORK QUICKLY BECAUSE IT DRIES VERY FAST. SMEAR A GOOD DOB ON EACH END OF THE STRIP, COVERING ABOUT 40 MM (1 1/2 IN) OF IT.

5 HOLDING THE SCREW, SLIP ONE END INTO THE HOLE, AND WORK IT ACROSS UNTIL THE OTHER END GETS IN. IF IT'S TOO LONG JUST TRIM A BIT OFF. CENTRE THE STRIP UP IN THE HOLE AND GENTLY PULL THE STRIP TOWARDS YOU.

80 mm (3 in)

80 mm (3 in)

hole in gyprock wall

70 mm (2 3/4 in)

replacement gyprock

screw

cornice cement

130 mm (5 in)

plastering

6 Your cornice cement should still be quite wet. Work any excess cement around the edges of the hole so that you bond the strip to the edge.

7 Hold the screw for about 2–3 minutes. The strip will be cemented to the inside of the hole.

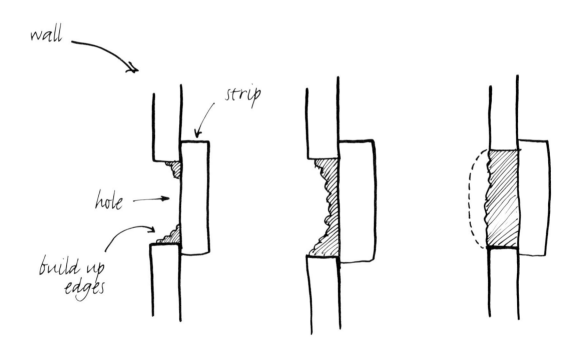

wall

strip

hole

build up edges

8 AFTER ABOUT AN HOUR, START BUILDING THE HOLE UP WITH CORNICE CEMENT UNTIL IT IS JUST SHORT OF BEING FULL — ABOUT 2 MM (1/10 IN).

9 BUY A 1 L (2 PT) CONTAINER OF PRE-MIXED TOP COAT. WAIT A COUPLE OF HOURS FOR THE CORNICE CEMENT TO GO OFF, THEN APPLY THE TOP COAT USING A SCRAPER THAT'S WIDER THAN THE HOLE. HOLD THE SCRAPER ON ABOUT A 45-DEGREE ANGLE AND RUN IT DOWN THE WALL OVER THE HOLE. LEAVE THE TOP COAT A LITTLE THICK AS IT'S EASY TO SAND OFF.

10 UNDERCOAT THE PATCH WITH A SEALER, THEN PAINT IT TO MATCH THE REST OF THE WALL.

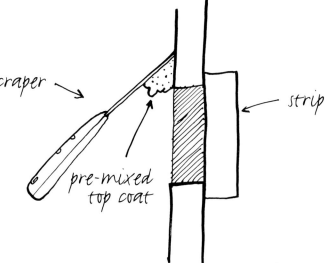

scraper

pre-mixed top coat

strip

Bernie's holiday

Bernie and the bride eventually had a couple of kiddies and they were one big happy family. I was always a bit worried for the kiddies if Bernie was knocking about with them — you never knew what injuries he was gonna cause them.

They went off on their family holiday down the south coast in a rented holiday house with Chook and his missus. The League Test Match was going to be on while they were down there, so Bernie and Chook had planned that to be the highlight of their trip.

About three days in, life was good, the Girls were getting on, weather was great, beers were flowing, only one small hiccup — the bushfires were in the area, albeit a fair hike away. They were in the back of Bernie's mind, specially with the two kids in tow.

Then conditions changed and the fires were on the move, right towards the holiday shack. Chook, being a bit of an expert on just about everything, said, 'Everything's sweet. The late arvo winds are going to switch around to the north-east. The fire will turn back on itself. We're not moving.'

Bernie was in two minds. He didn't know what to do — stay, go, stay, go. The local bushfire boys turned up and said, 'Everyone, you must evacuate now! Get on the bus!'

Bernie almost knocked the bloke over getting on the bus, then slowed down and got off. He got the kids and the wife. They were all packed on. Chook's standing at the door, saying, 'You can jam it. I'm not going. She's gonna swing around to the north-east and burn out.'

You gotta give it to the bloke for believing in his own bullshit. Here's the fire boys who live in the area saying, 'You must get out now!!!' And there's Chook saying, 'The Test is on tonight and I'm not budging.'

Chook stayed with his wife, and Bernie took off in the bus to shelter. They wacked Bernie and the family in the RSL Club for the night, all crowded in, everyone with sleeping bags and candles. No power, which means no Test.

Chook's at home watching the Test, drinking all of Bernie's beer, waiting for the wind to switch.

Incredibly, the wind switches to the north-east and runs back across the fire, away from the house.

Now it's heading for the RSL. Bernie's shitting bricks. They're wacked in the Rissole for the night with 200 screaming kids, and now it's going to burn down, and Chook's at home drinking all his beer.

Then Bernie and the rest of the mob were evacuated to a naval base and the Rissole burnt to the ground. They were stuck at the base for the next two days, and then finally made it back to the house — where Chook had drunk all the beer, his missus had polished off all of the bride's wine, and together they'd cleaned out all the food.

And Chook met them at the door and said, 'I told ya so.'

plastering

Job 2 SETTING GYPROCK

Problem YOU WANT TO PUT UP SOME GYPROCK SHEETING.

Solution TO HAVE ANY CHANCE OF DOING THIS RIGHT, YOU'VE GOT TO KNOW YOUR LIMITATIONS. SETTING GYPROCK TAKES A LOT OF PRACTICE, SO BE REALISTIC 'CAUSE EVEN MY MOTHER CAN PICK A BAD GYPROCK JOB. IT STANDS OUT LIKE DOG BALLS ON A CANARY.

YOU SHOULD START OFF HAVING A GO AT SETTING A RECESSED JOINT FIRST. THE GYPROCK COMES WITH THE RECESS SO IT CAN TAKE THE FILLER.

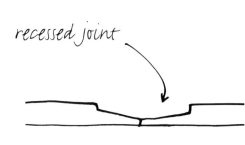

recessed joint

1 YOU'LL NEED JOINTING TAPE. USE EASY TAPE, WHICH IS A MESH THAT GOES OVER THE JOINT LIKE STICKY TAPE. KEEP IT WITHIN THE RECESS.

2 USING BASE COAT, PUT YOUR FIRST LAYER OF PLASTER ON, THEN FILL THE RECESS BY GOING ACROSS THE JOIN WITH A JOINTING KNIFE.

3 Holding the knife on a 45-degree angle, go down the join, scraping up the excess (you can buy a cheap plastic jointing knife that'll do the job).

4 Clean up all the edges and dags, and leave room for more plaster — don't get carried away and overfill the recess. Base coat is hard to sand when it's gone off.

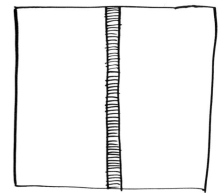

taping the join

5 Let that dry overnight. Then repeat the process with top coat. It's pre-mixed, and goes on nice and smooth if you have the right action. Just very, very slightly overfill the recess. When the top coat has gone off, lightly sand over the joint and presto, you're a gyprocker...well, sort of.

jointing knife

6 Next, seal the gyprock with an undercoat sealer before painting it. Ask the bloke at the paint shop what you need.

The stew

I worked for this bloke building shearing sheds in the bush. We'd be a week building the sheds then a week back at his property. When we were away — which was sometimes five to six hours' drive — his dear old wife would make these stews and casseroles. She'd freeze them in old ice cream containers, then on the Saturday when we were leaving for the week away, they'd go into the boot of the boss's car for the trip up, and that was our dinner for the week.

There were four of us, so I wasn't Robinson Crusoe when it came to bagging her cooking. It didn't help that it was 40° C and the food was sitting in the boot for five hours. Then it was put into an on-site fridge that we had on the back of the ute. And we're talking gear that doesn't react well to these conditions — cod casserole, tuna stew, steak and kidney stew, salmon casserole, curried sausage stews, and something else with tuna that no one wanted to know about. The same food every week and on the same days. So we knew on a Tuesday it was cod casserole, and that there'd be a queue for the crapper all day Wednesday! The boss never cottoned on it was his missus's cooking. 'Jeez, you blokes shit a lot.'

Now I eat anything — just about anything that's served up — and I always appreciate someone cooking for me, but this stuff tasted like boiled dog shit, and most of the time it sent us to the long drop. The only thing that helped us was the good ol' fashioned tommy sauce. In the end the boss had to buy the big four-litre plastic containers of the stuff. We'd drown this crap in tommy sauce just so it would slide down.

The boss used to say to us, 'Jeez, you blokes like ya sauce, don't ya!'

Job 3 PUTTING A VENT IN A GYPROCK WALL

Problem IF YOU NEED SOME VENTILATION THROUGH A GYPROCK WALL, A VENT IS THE GO.

Solution SIMPLE, TOO EASY.

1 FIRSTLY, MAKE SURE THERE ARE NO STUDS WHERE YOU WANT THE VENT. HAVE A BIT OF A TAP AROUND AND TRY TO GET BETWEEN TWO STUDS.

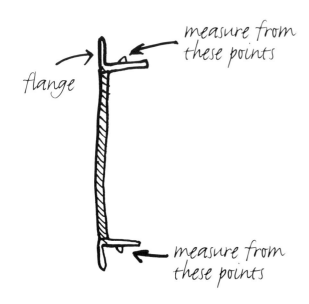

measure from these points

flange

measure from these points

cross-section of wall vent

2 YOUR VENT HAS A FLANGE OR LIP WHICH WILL COVER UP YOUR CUT EDGE.

3 SIT THE VENT ON THE WALL WITH A LEVEL AND MARK OUT THE PERIMETER OF THE VENT ON THE INSIDE. YOU CAN GET THE PENCIL IN THERE ON AN ANGLE UNDER THE FLANGE.

4 RUN ROUND THE PENCIL LINE WITH A STANLEY KNIFE, THEN DRILL A HOLE IN THE CENTRE.

5 WITH A HACKSAW BLADE, CUT FROM THE CENTRE OUT TO THE STANLEY KNIFE CUT. DO THIS AS MANY TIMES AS YOU NEED TO.

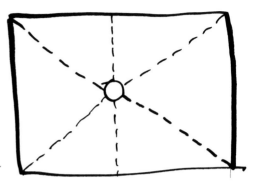

marking out position of vent

6 NOW JUST KNOCK THE TRIANGLE WITH YOUR KNUCKLE — IT'LL POP IN. CUT THE PAPER AT THE BACK WITH THE STANLEY UNTIL THE OPENING IS COMPLETE.

7 LINE THE VENT UP. GIVE HER AN OPEN-HANDED SLAP AND IN SHE GOES.

Glazing

Glazing scares me. When I carry glass or work with it, I'm always waiting for it to break. Most people have one phobia in their lives — spiders, heights. I think mine must be glassabreakerphobia. When you work with sheets of glass, just be aware of the dangers — a sliver of glass falling from waist height can be very nasty. Apart from all that, I love the stuff!

glazing

Job 1 REPLACING GLASS IN A TIMBER WINDOW

Problem WHEN I WAS A KID, HOW MANY TIMES DID I KICK THE FOOTY AND AS SOON AS IT LEFT MY BOOT, I KNEW...I'D JUST START RUNNING IN THE OTHER DIRECTION AND THE GLASS BUSTED AS I WAS RUNNING. WHEN I HIT THE CRICKET BALL AND IT WAS HEADING FOR THE WINDOW, I'D WILL IT AWAY FROM THE GLASS BY LEANING MY WHOLE BODY TO ONE SIDE. RIGHT ON IMPACT I'D STRAIGHTEN UP AND JUMP AT THE SAME TIME, SAYING 'SHIT!' BEFORE HIGHTAILING IT OUT OF THERE.

Solution I WOULDN'T HAVE A GO AT FIXING A WINDOW ANY BIGGER THAN A STANDARD DOUBLE-HUNG WINDOW, ABOUT 600 x 600 MM (2 x 2 FT). GLASS IS VERY DANGEROUS AND BIG STUFF SHOULD BE LEFT TO THE PROS.

1 IT'S MUCH EASIER TO REPAIR THE GLASS WITH THE WINDOW SASH OUT OF ITS FRAME AND ON A WORKBENCH. IF THIS IS TOO HARD FOR YOU, JUST FIX IT WHILE IT'S IN POSITION.

2 Always have gloves on. Break out all the old glass. Hopefully the old putty will pop out with the glass, but there's always some left. Chip out all the old putty and any nails so that the rebate where the glass sits is back to timber.

3 Measure the opening for the new glass. For a nice easy fit, allow about 2 mm ($^{1}/_{10}$ in) all the way round.

4 Drop in your glass. Now you'll need push points, available at any hardware store. These hold the glass in place before the putty goes on.

5 Lay the push points flat side down on the glass. Sitting a chisel on the edge at the back (opposite end to the points), slide the push point over to the timber frame and give a little tap with a hammer until each one is home.

push point

glazing

6 GLAZING PUTTY NEEDS TO BE LIKE PLAY DOUGH. WORK IT IN YOUR HANDS UNTIL IT'S ALL THE SAME CONSISTENCY. OVERFILL THE REBATE ALL THE WAY AROUND — GET A BIG LUMP IN YOUR HAND AND PUSH IT ACROSS THE REBATE.

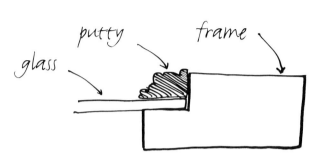

glass

putty

frame

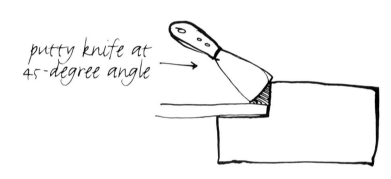

putty knife at 45-degree angle

7 RUN THE PUTTY KNIFE ALONG THE PUTTY AT A 45-DEGREE ANGLE, PUSHING DOWN HARD. THIS TAKES SOME PRACTICE — JUST KEEP ADDING PUTTY TO THE LOW SPOTS AND KEEP KNIFING IT SMOOTH. YOU'LL BE RIGHT.

The edger blade

While working in a resort in north-western Australia, I was given the job of maintenance manager. I ran half a dozen blokes who did the lawns, gardens, rubbish collection and so on. At the time, this was a big job for me. I was a young bloke and keen to impress — especially the boss, the general manager of the resort who gave me the job.

Barry and I were standing in the pool area, discussing a problem with the filtration system. There were about six families playing in the pool. It was a hot day and everyone was having a great time. Bazza was very happy with the way I was handling things. I was chest out and bloody bulletproof.

One of the guests came over to have a chat with us. I was standing next to Barry with the guest facing us. Then suddenly, out of the sky, without warning, travelling about 1000 miles an hour, came a flat piece of steel about six inches long, flipping end over end. It just shaved past the guest's head and hit Bazza right in the bicep, knocking him clean over. He was lying there beside me with this piece of steel hanging out of his arm.

I actually saw it coming out of the sky — saw it curling around towards us like a Terry Alderman outswinger. If it had hit the guest in the head, it would have been 'Good night, Irene'.

Bazza was rolling on the ground, screaming, 'What the f*** was that!!!' Because I had neglected to save him by pushing him out of the way and diving in to take the bullet, I thought I'd better find out who did it.

I ran out of the pool area, asking guests and workers

158

if they'd seen anything. I bumped into Robby, one of the labourers, doing the edges on the lawn about 500 metres away from the pool. He's on his hands and knees looking through the grass around the edging machine.

'What are ya doing, Rob?'

'Well, the edger blade's fallen off. I'm just looking for it.'

On the top of the guard around the edger was a perfect slot where the blade had punched through. It must have shaved his right ear, then flown the 500 metres. And what are the odds — about 10 million to one? — it lands on the boss's arm.

Nice one!

Job 2 CUTTING GLASS

Problem NEED TO CUT A BIT OF GLASS FOR THAT PICTURE FRAME.

Solution START WITH PICTURE-FRAME GLASS, WHICH IS ABOUT 3 MM ($^1/_{10}$ IN) THICK. THIS WILL GIVE YOU A BIT OF AN IDEA HOW GLASS-CUTTING WORKS. IT'S QUITE EASY TO CUT 3 MM ($^1/_{10}$ IN).

1 YOU'LL NEED A GLASS CUTTER. THERE'RE OIL-FILLED ONES WHICH ARE QUITE EXPENSIVE BUT FOR 3 MM ($^1/_{10}$ IN) YOU'LL GET AWAY WITH A CHEAPY. ASK YOUR HARDWARE STORE MAN.

2 LAY A RULER ON YOUR GLASS, LINE UP THE CUTTING WHEEL WITH YOUR LINE, PUSH DOWN FIRMLY AND PULL THE CUTTER TOWARDS YOU.

3 THE WHEEL WILL LEAVE A WHITE LINE ON THE GLASS. WHACK A MATCH IN EACH END UNDER THE CUT LINE SO THE GLASS IS SEESAWING ON THE MATCHES. PUSH DOWN ON THE ADJACENT EDGES, AND SNAP...YOU'VE CUT GLASS.

glass cutter

matchsticks
glass

snapping glass

KIDDIES AND GLASS

I REMEMBER A KID AT SCHOOL WHEN I WAS A TACKER — BRETT C. HE WAS OFF SICK FOR A WHILE. WHEN HE CAME BACK, HE LOOKED LIKE HE'D BEEN IN A KNIFE FIGHT WITH THE RUSSIAN MAFIA. SCARS ALL OVER HIM. HE'D JUMPED THROUGH A BIG WINDOW.

SO, IS THERE A SOLUTION? AT MY PLACE, I PULLED THE OLD GLASS OUT OF ALL THE WINDOWS THAT THE KIDS COULD REACH — WHETHER THEY WERE AT GROUND LEVEL OR COULD BE REACHED BY STANDING ON THE COUCH — AND HAD LAMINATED GLASS, COMMONLY KNOWN AS SAFETY GLASS, PUT IN. THIS IS A BIT MORE EXPENSIVE THAN NORMAL GLASS.

LAMINATED GLASS IS TWO SHEETS OF GLASS STUCK TOGETHER WITH A CLEAR PLASTIC FILM, SORT OF LIKE CONTACT PAPER, IN THE MIDDLE.

IF YOU RUN AT A FRENCH DOOR WHICH HAS SAFETY GLASS...FIRSTLY, YOU MIGHT NOT BREAK IT, IT'S PRETTY TOUGH. BUT IF IT DID BREAK, IT SHATTERS AND STAYS IN PLACE — THERE'S NO WAY YOU COULD GO THROUGH IT — AND YOU END UP WITH A BIG SPIDER WEB PATTERN IN THE GLASS.

Job 3 BROKEN PICTURE-FRAME GLASS

Problem IF YOUR PICTURE'S FALLEN OFF THE WALL, GO BACK TO THE CHAPTER ON CARPENTRY AND FIND OUT HOW TO HANG IT PROPERLY (SEE JOB 16, 'HANGING A PICTURE').

Solution 1 ROLL THE PICTURE FRAME OVER AND CUT THE MASKING TAPE WITH A STANLEY KNIFE.

2 YOU'LL USUALLY FIND SMALL PUSH POINTS LIKE ARROWHEADS OR NAILS HOLDING THE PICTURE, MOUNT BOARD AND GLASS IN PLACE. POP THEM OUT AND TRY TO SAVE THEM.

3 NOW THAT YOU KNOW HOW TO CUT 3 MM (1/10 IN) GLASS (SEE JOB 2, 'CUTTING GLASS'), MEASURE UP. LAY ALL THE PIECES BACK IN THE FRAME, WACK IN THE PUSH POINTS AND TAPE UP THE JOIN.

4 PUT THE CORRECT PICTURE HOOK IN THE WALL AND IT WON'T HAPPEN AGAIN.

SOME ROOFING OPTIONS

BEFORE WE FIND AN ALTERNATIVE, REMEMBER — IF YOU'RE PUTTING IN A GLASS ROOF, NORTH-FACING IS PROBABLY THE BEST. FOR A WEST-FACING ROOF, BE PREPARED FOR VERY HOT SUN BLAZING IN; ON THE SOUTH, EXPECT VERY LITTLE. CHECK FOR BIG OVERHANGING TREES 'CAUSE THEY CAUSE LOTS OF GRIEF ON A GLASS ROOF — ESPECIALLY GUM TREES, AS THEY DROP PLENTY OF LEAVES WHICH STAIN THE GLASS. YOU'RE FOREVER UP THERE CLEANING THE GLASS AND IF THERE'S TIMBER INVOLVED, A BUILDUP OF LEAVES LEFT FOR A LONG TIME HOLDS MOISTURE, WHICH KEEPS THE TIMBER MOIST, WHICH THEN CAUSES THE TIMBER TO ROT.

GETTING BACK TO GLASS — ONE GOOD ALTERNATIVE IS POLYCARBONATE. IT'S A PLASTIC AND COMES IN LARGER SHEETS, THEREFORE YOU HAVE FEWER JOINS. IT'S A BIT CHEAPER BUT IN MY OPINION MUCH EASIER TO INSTALL — COMPARE THE PRICES AND SEE HOW YOU GO.

Electrical

I'm not going to beat around the bush here. 240 volts can kill you. So get a sparky. Treat every wire you find as live — in other words, there are 240 volts running through it. Even if you think the power could not possibly be on, treat it as if it is. This chapter is tiny, and for good reason. The knucklehead has virtually nothing in common with 240 volts. So if you have an electrical problem, call a sparky!

Job 1 CHANGING THE FLUORO

Problem YOUR FLUORESCENT LIGHT IS EITHER FLICKERING, OR NOT WORKING AT ALL.

Solution TO THE BLOKE WHO'S DONE THIS BEFORE, IT SOUNDS SIMPLE. BUT THERE'S NOTHING MORE ANNOYING THAN THE FLICKERING FLUORO. IF THE LIGHT IS COMPLETELY DEAD, YOU'LL NEED A NEW TUBE.

1 BEFORE YOU DO ANYTHING, GO ROUND TO YOUR ELECTRICAL BOX, WHICH IS OUT THE FRONT OR ROUND THE SIDE, AND TURN THE MAIN SWITCH OFF. GO INSIDE, AND CHECK THE OTHER LIGHTS AND ANY DIGITAL CLOCKS TO MAKE SURE YOU'VE HIT THE RIGHT SWITCH.

2 TAKE THE COVER OFF. SOMETIMES THERE ARE TWO SCREWS AT EITHER END HOLDING THE CAPS ON, WHICH IN TURN HOLD THE COVER ON. YOU SHOULD BE ABLE TO TAKE ONE OFF AND POP THE COVER OFF TO REVEAL THE TUBE.

3 GRAB THE TUBE AND ROTATE IT SLIGHTLY, PULLING ON IT. THE TUBE WILL POP OUT.

4 WITH THE NEW TUBE, LINE UP THE LUGS WITH THE SLOT AT EACH END. SLIDE THE LUGS IN AND ROTATE THE TUBE. IT IS NOW LOCKED OFF AND READY TO TEST.

THE OTHER THING THAT CAN GO WRONG WITH FLUOROS IS THE STARTER. THESE ARE SMALL WHITE CYLINDERS POKING OUT FROM THE LIGHT BODY. THEY LOOK A BIT LIKE PLASTIC FILM CANISTERS, ONLY SMALLER. IF THE NEW TUBE IS IN BUT THE LIGHT IS STILL FLICKERING, YOU NEED TO REPLACE THE STARTERS.

starter

1 JUST PUSH UP SLIGHTLY AND TURN THE STARTER. IT WILL POP OUT.

2 REPLACE IT AND SEE HOW YOU GO. IF YOU'RE STILL HAVING PROBLEMS, LEAVE IT AT THAT AND CALL THE SPARKY.

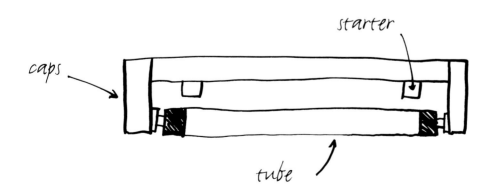

starter

caps

tube

Job 2 POWER HAS GONE OUT

Problem YOU'RE SETTLING DOWN IN FRONT OF THE TELLY FOR THE GRAND FINAL AND THE POWER GOES OFF. BETTER FIX IT IN A HURRY.

Solution IT DEPENDS ON WHAT YOU'VE GOT IN YOUR METER BOX. YOU MIGHT HAVE THE OLD CERAMIC FUSES OR THE NEW BREAKERS.

ceramic fuses

breakers

Fuses

1 TURN OFF THE MAIN SWITCH. POP OUT THE CERAMIC FUSE AND CHECK TO SEE IF THE WIRE RUNNING THROUGH IT IS BROKEN. IF IT IS, THE FUSE HAS BLOWN.

2 JUST UNDO THE SCREWS ENOUGH TO REMOVE
THE WIRE AND REPLACE IT WITH THE SAME SIZE.
THE AMP SIZE OF THE WIRE IS WRITTEN
ON THE FUSE — FOR EXAMPLE, 20A, 8A.

fuse

Breakers

POP IT BACK AND TURN THE MAIN ON. IF
THE FUSE BLOWS AGAIN, GET A SPARKY.

IF YOU HAVE THE NEW SYSTEM — WITH
BREAKERS — IT'S SIMPLE. ALL YOUR SWITCHES
SHOULD BE ON. WHEN YOU OPEN THE METER
BOX UP, LOOK FOR THE BREAKER THAT HAS
TRIPPED TO OFF. JUST TURN IT ON. IF IT TRIPS
AGAIN TO OFF, CALL A SPARKY.

Mutton steaks

I was in between houses while living in Fremantle, Western Australia, and accommodation was hard to come by 'cause the America's Cup had been on and heaps of backpackers stayed in town, filling up all the rooms to rent.

I was going through the ads in the paper and there was bugger all. But I found this great room in a house close to the beach — open fireplace and cheap as chips. The ad read: 'Non-drinking, non-smoking vegetarian wanted.'

That's me. I rang up and set up an interview. It was two girls. They were living alternatively — a bit bohemian. At least, that's what it sounded like on the phone.

So I got some sandals and a tie-dyed shirt, and practised slowing my speech down and dropping a few decibels. All that alternative mob talk like they add Prozac to their cereal.

When I arrived the Girls fell for it hook, line and sinker. They loved me and I moved in straightaway.

We spent that afternoon listening to Joan Baez and Bob Dylan LPs, with me saying every second song, 'This one's a classic.'

The next morning I woke up and wandered around the house, up and down searching for the telly. There was no telly. Who the hell lives without telly? I couldn't stand another night of folk music — I'd end up stringing myself from the garage rafters.

Straight on the blower to Radio Rentals. 'Get us a 53-inch stat. The footsa's coming on this arvo.' I told the Girls, 'I'm a big fan of the SBS docos and wouldn't dare watch that commercial crap. Even the ABC has a lot to answer for.' The Girls agreed.

United we stand. 'Hey,

hey,' we all laughed and cheered...I nearly chundered.

Anyway I had a cheap room and a telly. I just needed to get the case of grog into the camp fridge I had set up at the end of my bed.

Things were going great. The Girls worked shift work in some carrot juice café, so I was able to slip off to the pub, and then pop home with a few cans and watch that commercial crap we all hated so much.

This went on for a while, until the wheels started falling off. They were on to me. They started to realise I wasn't the didgeridoo-playing freak I was making out to be. They got very nasty. Basically they despised everything I lived for. It got to the point where they ganged up, abusing me, making fun. You could cut the air with a knife.

What they hated most was meat in the house. I used to have a counter meal most nights, but I've been a steak, chips and egg with black sauce bloke since I can remember, but at home, in front of the telly.

So I figured, 'This is restriction of trade.' Straight to the butcher. 'Half a lamb, thanks champ.' Took the little fella home, put on the white apron, got out my carpentry tool box and started cutting up my leg o'lambs, chops and cutlets — all with the Spear & Jackson handsaw and the hacksaw. I had the hammer and chisel out at one stage. I'm no butcher, so it was rough as canvas undies, but I was doing the job. One thing, though. It looked like I'd slaughtered a horse in the kitchen. The room reserved for eggplant and tofu had been turned into a boning yard.

The Girls came home and both of them nearly had coronaries. They were horrified. I packed up my meat, cleaned up and said, 'Well, I think my work here is done. I'll be off.'

I've never seen the Girls since but I bet they're married with three tackers each, cooking bloody big T-bones for all the family...maybe not.

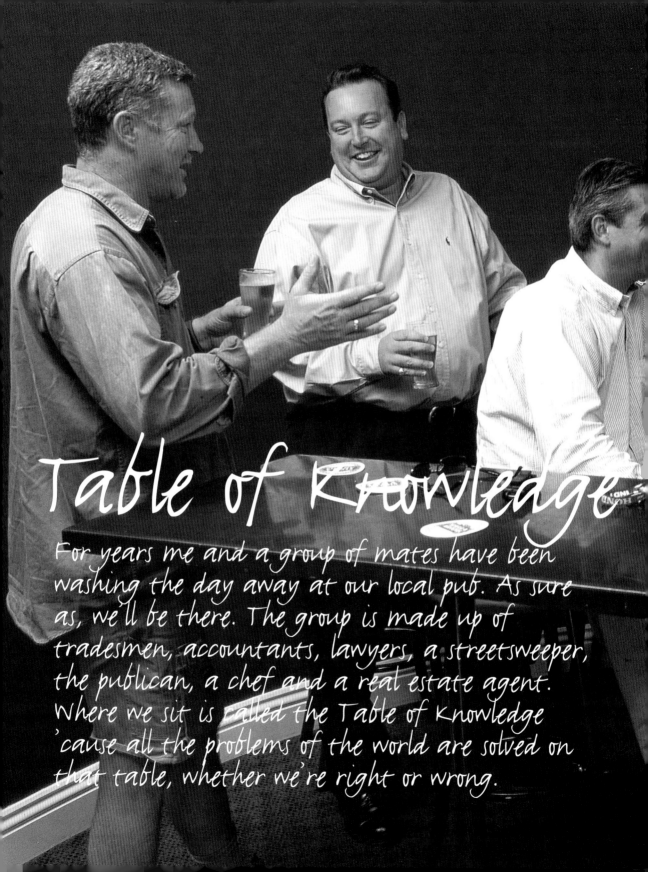

Table of Knowledge

For years me and a group of mates have been
washing the day away at our local pub. As sure
as, we'll be there. The group is made up of
tradesmen, accountants, lawyers, a streetsweeper,
the publican, a chef and a real estate agent.
Where we sit is called the Table of Knowledge
'cause all the problems of the world are solved on
that table, whether we're right or wrong.

The garage

Besides the Table of Knowledge, the patrons in our local pub vary. A couple of gay blokes, funeral directors and bus drivers go between us and the locals. You've got just about everything covered. The two fellas who putt out of the rough are great blokes who I get on with, no problem. Each to his own.

One day the Table of Knowledge was trying to solve a problem for Bryan, a carpenter mate of mine

looking for a rental garage close by to store his tools in. We're all saying, 'What about Bernie?' 'No, he's got a boat.' Everyone was rattling off names.

I looked over and saw Phil, one of the rough putters I knew, sitting on his own. I knew neither he nor his partner owned a car and they lived only a block from the pub. Most of the joints around here have garages up the back, but I didn't know if Phil and Tony had a lane up the back of their terrace for a garage 'cause, as I said, 'They're great blokes, but it doesn't mean I've been to their house.'

Phil was sitting in the opposite corner from the Table of Knowledge and I was excited that I'd solved the problem.

Just as things went a little quiet, with Phil not having a clue what we're talking about, I screamed out across the

bar, 'Hey, Phil, you got rear access, mate?' The whole joint looked at me, including the barmaid I'd been chatting up.

And Phil said, 'Not for you, Scotty.'

Needless to say, my shout at the Table.

BUILDING MYTHS AND LEGENDS

1 THE WATER STORAGE UNIT ABOVE THE TOILET IS A CISTERN, NOT A SYSTEM.

2 240 VOLTS CAN KILL YOU. GET A SPARKY.

3 CLIMBING A TREE WITH A CHAINSAW IS THE BEST WAY TO CUT YOUR ARM OFF...IF YOU NEED TO.

4 SPRAYING AIR FRESHENER IN THE DUNNY JUST MAKES THE DUNNY SMELL LIKE AIR FRESHENER AND SHIT.

5 LIGHTING A MATCH DOESN'T WORK EITHER.

6 IF YOU ASK YOUR WIFE OR HUSBAND TO HELP YOU WITH SOME HANDYMAN WORK, YOU'LL END UP HAVING A STINK...IT'S A KNOWN FACT.

7 BEER ALWAYS TASTES BETTER AFTER A HARD DAY ON THE TOOLS...ANOTHER FACT.

8 If something is proving too tough to lift or undo...it's all in the expression on your face — the further the vein in your neck pops out, the better chance you've got.

9 Blokes in work boots and flannos meet more women...I made that one up.

10 Good sorts driving utes...well, you just can't beat it.

11 If you don't have a bacon and egg roll for smoko, you're doing it all wrong.

WHAT TO WEAR OUT

When you've finished your weekend jobs, it's time to take the missus out for a bite. But you still want to look the part. Wear your best flanno shirt (ironed), and clean work shorts and boots, then with your faithful dog in the back of the ute, hit the local pub.

ironed flanno shirt

clean work shorts

faithful dog

clean elastic-sided
work boots

INDEX

index